The BERTON FAMILY Cookbook

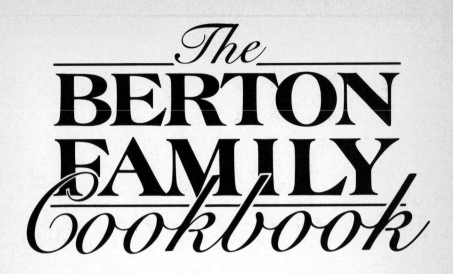

The BERTON FAMILY Cookbook

Foreword by
Pierre Berton

Introduction by
Janet Berton

Edited by
Paul Berton

Recipes by (in the order they're counted for dinner):

Pierre Berton
Janet Berton
Penny Berton
John Hardy
Elora Berton Hardy
Pamela Berton
Patsy Berton

Rico Gerussi
Liam Berton Gerussi
Peter Berton
Paula Berton
Eric Basciano
Paul Berton
Peggy Anne Berton
Perri Berton

The BERTON FAMILY Cookbook

Conceived by
John Hardy

Co-ordinated and Compiled by
Penny Berton

Cartoons by
Patsy Berton

Additional Drawings by
Peter Berton
and
Peggy Anne Berton

Copy Reading by
Pamela Berton

Courier Services by
Perri Berton

McClelland and Stewart

The Canadian Publishers
McClelland and Stewart Limited
25 Hollinger Road, Toronto M4B 3G2

Canadian Cataloguing in Publication Data

Main entry under title:
The Berton family cookbook

Includes index.
ISBN 0-7710-1227-6

1. Cookery. 2. Berton family. I. Berton, Penny.
II. Berton, Paul.

TX715.B47 1985   641.5   C85-099609-0

Printed in Canada

Contents

Foreword

Pierre Berton

A few years ago, on our wedding anniversary, our children presented Janet and me with a unique gift. They arrived at the house laden down with packages, moved into the kitchen, and proceeded to organize and cook a seven-course gourmet dinner. I can think of no better anniversary: not just because of the menu, which was superb, but because of the symbolism. Each of them had a job to do: one prepared the hors d'oeuvres, another the drinks, a third the soup, a fourth the salad, and so on right down to the Grand Marnier soufflé. In short, our children had learned much more than the art of good cooking; they had learned teamwork, organization, and leadership.

Since then, we have made a ritual out of anniversary dinners as, indeed, we make a ritual out of most festive days. All through history, rites of passage have been marked by the preparation and enjoyment of food: birthdays, Christmas, anniversaries, Thanksgivings, celebrations of all kinds – yes, even funerals. Our family believes in ritual; it is the glue that holds any community together – the acting out, in common, of a tribal rite. For us, this common activity takes place in the kitchen and around the dining room table.

We celebrate all feast days – with a feast, naturally. We never miss a birthday and we always have a cake with candles. We have full-moon parties in which everybody dresses in white and eats marshmallows and popcorn. We never miss out on pumpkin pie at Thanksgiving. Christmas Eve and Boxing Day produce their own attractions, listed in the pages that follow.

Janet's kitchen has always been open to anyone of the family or friends who wants to use it – whether they're indulging in a cheese dream at 2 A.M. or making shirred eggs for Sunday-morning breakfast. This requires considerable give-and-take: only one person can use the wok, or the food processor, or the mixing machine, or the pastry board at a time. And give-and-take, which is another word for organization, is all part of family cooking.

The family learned organization on holidays. We've spent our vacations on the islands in the Gulf of Georgia, on a rubber raft down the Yukon river, in villas in the Caribbean. Early in the game we learned teamwork. I remember on Galiano Island, for instance, we divided the work among three teams. One team cooked. One did the dishes. One cleaned up the cottage. Each day we shifted the teams around so the work was evenly divided. And, of course, the cooking team had the most fun. They were given a sum of money and *carte blanche* to find the food, prepare the menus, cook and serve the dishes. We've used that system ever since and I recommend it to all groups who go camping.

It's not been easy to put this book together because it's not been easy to figure out the quantities. Our family cooks by the tongue; we taste and taste and taste until the dish is right. Now we've had to measure by teaspoon and cupful and that's been a drag. And so, when preparing the dishes in this book, remember that the quantities are not necessarily engraved in stone. We've tested them but you should test them, too – with your palate. You may not like rice as spicy as Penny does; you may not like corned beef hash as piquant as I do; you may not want to put so much garlic into some of the dishes here. Change things around; invent; explore. That's how we all learned to cook.

We've always encouraged our children to try new dishes, and with the possible exception of cold parsnip sandwiches, they've been willing to attempt anything. Now that they've done some travelling, the shoe is on the other foot. They come back from places like Bangkok and Bali and urge new concoctions on us stay-at-homes. That may explain the prominence of curry and ginger in so many of the recipes that follow.

One thing we learned early is that when you're raising kids in the kitchen, you've got to give them their head. Let them try things and make their own mistakes. Don't stand over them and lay down the law. Help, advise, show: but don't order. *And don't do it for them!* They have to learn the hard way. Our four-year-old granddaughter is already making what she calls "puffed eggs." So she scrambles them in an odd way! So what? Before long she'll be into soufflés. Every one of us learned by trial and error, by tasting, by making mistakes; that's the fun of it. And cooking, like eating, ought to be fun. Remember: the family that sautés together, stays together!

7

Introduction

Janet Berton

In 1966, when Pierre and I produced the *Canadian Centennial Food Guide*, a history of Canadian cooking, there were very few cookbooks around. (Our grandmothers kept their favourite "receipts" from friends and neighbours in old scribblers, cherishing them like the family silver. Some women even went to the grave without revealing their culinary secrets.)

Today, immigration and travel have sparked an interest in exotic foods, and whole bookstores are devoted to cookbooks alone. It seems that every church group and charitable organization in the country is compiling favourite recipes.

This book is a collection of favourite recipes from each member of the family. Included are some old Canadian standbys like butter tarts, rarely mentioned in American cookbooks. Pioneer recipes for bear steaks and beaver-tail soup are noticeably missing here. Instead there are suggestions for the modern family or any group trying to cope with the fact that everyone is working outside the home, but would still like to prepare some meals in a co-operative way.

In our family the kitchen has always been a focal point. In the early days the refrigerator was the first piece of real equipment we bought, and it sat proudly in the middle of the bare living room. (The kitchen didn't have a floor yet – just gravel.) Nowadays, the children, all grown, rush to the fridge the minute they walk in the door on the weekends. There's always something to nibble on there, they point out. It's also the place we, like most families, put our notes, grocery lists, phone messages, and children's drawings. It seems that the fridge has replaced the hearth as the centre of the modern home and has become the source of nourishment, spiritually and physically.

We enlarged the kitchen some years ago. Since then we have found that it's a lot more fun to prepare meals together because there is a large central counter where we all can work at once. Not everyone has this advantage, but it's important, we think, for families at least to eat together – to share ideas, to learn to listen to the next person – rather than for everyone to heat up their frozen food in a microwave as they rush off on different schedules.

A family friend remarked that we always seem to be able to take on one more for dinner without much difficulty. That's because with dishes like soup or stew it's easy to add a little more. Soup has always been a mainstay in our household; Pierre likes homemade soup with every dinner. If we have extra guests at the last minute, we blend some leftover vegetables into the soup or add a can of tomatoes and some herbs.

We laugh now about one of the rare times we had a real black tie dinner complete with hired help. I had made a beet borscht and strained it so that it would be crystal clear. Although I had measured it carefully, the servings were apparently too big. After only half the twenty guests had been served, the waiter whispered to me that we were running out. I ran to the kitchen, rescued the beets and vegetables I had strained out and thriftily tucked into the fridge for the next day, threw them into the blender with a can of tomatoes and a bouillon cube dissolved in hot water, and added it to the rest. No one noticed the difference.

Canned tomatoes are one of the staples in our cupboard but generally we try to avoid processed foods. Pierre, however, says he still prefers canned spinach (grey) and canned peas (army green) as those were the only kinds there were in Dawson City, Yukon, in his youth. And, of course, it all brings back memories of his childhood.

Nonetheless, in keeping with new ideas about nutrition, we've been trying to modify our diet to contain less red meat and fat, less sugar, more fish, fresh vegetables and fruit, and more fibre. These recipes show some of the ways we have found to do this.

When the children were small, we went through a lot of peanut-butter sandwiches. Now they prefer more sophisticated fare, although in their own homes they eat more simply than we all do on weekends. On those occasions, everyone gets involved. This doesn't mean just chopping onions for the chef. It means preparing a whole dish and feeling a sense of pride and accomplishment – and involvement. The dishes pile up, the counter is a mess, and the drawers get clogged with bits of chopped vegetables. And, of course, there are times when there are disagreements about what we're having for dinner: "Roast beef again?" or "Oh, I felt like having chicken tonight," or "Why can't we have a barbecue instead?" or "Tofu and bean sprouts . . . ugh!"

But eventually it all comes together, and everyone feels the satisfaction of having contributed to the success of a festive occasion.

Many dinner guests have been amazed watching how much time our whole family spends planning menus, shopping for food, preparing meals – or eating them up. We finally realized that perhaps the way we share food preparation might interest other families and groups who eat together. It's easier on everybody; it makes for wonderful food – and it's a lot more fun.

General Notes

1. **Level of Difficulty**
   In each recipe, we have indicated the level of difficulty:
   Easy – ✗
   Intermediate – ✗✗
   Difficult – ✗✗✗

2. **Time**
   The preparation time indicated at the top of each recipe includes both preparation and cooking times for the average cook. These are approximate times and should be adjusted to your own pace. The term "overnight" is used to indicate that a dish should be chilled or prepared ahead of time.

3. **Preheat Oven**
   In recipes that use an oven, the oven should always be preheated.

4. **Ingredients**
   Tamari soy sauce: This is organically brewed Japanese soy sauce; it is lighter than the more common, less expensive Chinese soy sauce. We prefer the flavour, especially when it is sprinkled on rice or vegetables at the table. Tamari is available in health-food stores and some grocery stores.
   Tahini: This is a paste made of ground sesame seeds, available in natural-food stores and Middle Eastern shops.
   Sesame oil: This oil is really more a seasoning than a cooking oil. Add a little to your regular oil for frying or marinades — it contributes a special flavour to any dish.
   Toasted ground sesame seeds: We recommend these as a delicious and nutritious topping for rice and vegetables. Just toast in oven or wok (dry) until light brown and partially grind in blender to retain some crunch.

5. **Menus**
   The recipes for items preceded by an asterisk (*) appear in this book. Those in bold face appear directly after the menu.

About the Cooks

PENNY and her husband JOHN HARDY thought up this book. They live, eat, and design jewellery in Bali, Indonesia, so many of their recipes have a distinctly Southeast Asian flavour. Elora Jade, their four-year-old daughter, seems to live exclusively on rice and fish. As the eldest, Penny has always been the organizer, which may account for her work as compiler, organizer, and motivator for this book.

PAMELA is a naturalist. On hiking trips it's she who finds the wild onions, who makes jelly from May apples and vegetable soufflés from pig weed and thistles. She designs and cares for the family garden, the source of father's tomato soup, a summer favourite. As well, she once cultivated a thriving herb garden on the far hill in Kleinburg, and later sold kitchen herb mixtures under the label Freshfields. She organizes tours for the Federation of Ontario Naturalists.

PATSY, an artist and massage therapist, and her husband RICO GERUSSI, a musician, were vegetarians for years, but more recently they have been known to eat rare roast beef with Perri's Yorkshire pudding. Still, they prefer lighter foods with lots of vegetables. Their son, Liam, is already on a mostly vegetarian Pablum diet. As avid tea drinkers, they are forever creating the appropriate tea-time snacks.

PETER, an architect, and his wife PAULA, a teacher, are the entertainers. Peter is king of the hors d'œuvres. When we're all sitting around before dinner he'll arrive with a tray of curried crab on toast or some other delectable delicacy. He's also known for the quality and potency of his drinks: a Muskoka Sunrise has laid more than one good man down.

ERIC is a late-nighter. When most of the family is abed he's in the kitchen making cheese dreams, his acknowledged specialty, or some other unidentifiable dish. As his recipes reveal, he's a master at raiding the fridge for leftovers and creating something from the discards. Of course, in the dimly

Hamilton Beach Pierre Angus Janet Penny John Elora Paula Peter

12

lit atmosphere of early morning, food takes on a whole new quality. Eric's name doesn't start with a P because he arrived on his sixteenth birthday. Fifteen years later, he's still with us. As a university student, Eric is still honing his scotiobiotic culinary techniques.

PAUL is Mr. Orderly. He cannot enter a messy kitchen without scrubbing it down and arranging all the utensils and food for quick and easy operation. He's a master chef when it comes to fish. His steamed pickerel is ambrosia and his sauteed shrimps a masterpiece. With Peter he's also an expert barbecuer. His marinated chicken never burns and his steaks are always rare. He is a journalist.

PEGGY ANNE is an expert at cooking in a telephone booth on a minimum wage. As an animation student living in New York, she has perfected these skills in her telephone-booth-sized apartment.

PERRI (who came to us at seven months) is our dessert expert. She makes all the birthday cakes, Sunday morning crepes, and chocolate chip cookies. In fact, she taught her mother how to make pie crust, and the two of them are now making pies faster than they can be eaten. She is a university student.

FATHER makes hearty food, and when he enters the kitchen, panic breaks out. "He's in the kitchen!" warns Pamela as she frantically covers the floor in newspapers and puts an apron over father's best suit. "He's in the kitchen!" shouts Patsy, as the family beats a hasty retreat while father swings his giant cleaver and bits of potato and onion fly across the room. Nonetheless, his turkey croquettes get eaten to the last crumb on Boxing Day morning when no one else has the energy to lift a paring knife.

MOTHER taught us all. Half the recipes in this book (at least) are hers. She cooks instinctively, by taste, sight, and smell and had to be persuaded, with difficulty, to add exact quantities for the purposes of this book. The reason the whole family cooks is because Mother encouraged us to use the kitchen, to make mistakes, to gain a feeling of self-confidence, to learn to love food and prepare it properly by actually doing the work ourselves, without let or hindrance.

Eric   Paul   Pamela   Patsy   Liam   Rico   Perri   Peggy   Anne   Liddle Dave
                                            Rodney

13

BREAKFASTS

MENU

Mother's Day Breakfast

Stewed Rhubarb *by Pamela*

*"If You Love Ginger" Muffins *by Patsy*

*Apple-Cheese Pan Puffs *by Penny*

Crispy Bacon *by Peter*

Coffee

"If You Love Ginger" Muffins

Makes 12 muffins
Total time: 35 minutes

Patsy

When I experimented with this creation and asked for opinions, Peter and Paula found the ginger too overpowering, but Rico called me from work the next day and said, "Terrific muffins!" (And he doesn't even like apricots.)

    1 cup whole-wheat flour
    ¼ cup wheat germ
    ¼ cup bran
    3 tsp. baking powder
    ½ tsp. cinnamon
    ½ tsp. nutmeg (optional)
    2 eggs, beaten
    3 tbsp. brown sugar
    ¾ cup milk
    ¼ cup vegetable oil
    ⅔ cup cooked brown rice
    1 tbsp. grated fresh ginger (or 2 tsp. ground ginger)
    ½ cup chopped dried apricots or ½ cup raisins

1. In a very large bowl, mix together flour, wheat germ, bran, baking powder, cinnamon, and nutmeg.
2. In another bowl, mix eggs, brown sugar, milk, oil, cooked brown rice, grated ginger, and apricots.
3. Add the egg mixture to the flour and stir only enough to moisten.
4. Spoon batter into 12 well-greased muffin tins.
5. Bake in a 375 F oven for about 20 minutes.

Apple-Cheese Pan Puffs

Serves 4
Total time: 30 minutes **Penny**

One morning in Kleinburg, I announced my intention to make pancakes. Immediately a chorus of groans resulted, and everyone hastened to prepare eggs and bacon. But I made them anyway, and all I heard were cries for more. From then on, I've called them pan puffs instead of pancakes.

1 cup cottage cheese or 1 cup tofu, mashed
1 packed cup grated apple
¾ cup whole-wheat flour
1 tbsp. honey
1 tsp. lemon juice
2 tbsp. chopped cashews or almonds
1 tsp. cinnamon
½ tsp. nutmeg
½ tsp. salt
4 egg yolks
1 tbsp. grated orange rind
4 egg whites
Butter and oil for frying

1. In a large mixing bowl, combine cottage cheese, apple, flour, honey, lemon juice, chopped nuts, cinnamon, nutmeg, salt, and egg yolks.
2. In another bowl, beat egg whites until stiff, then fold gently into mixture in large bowl.
3. In a large cast-iron skillet, melt a little butter and oil.
4. Using a ¼-cup measure, drop batter into skillet. You should be able to fry several puffs at once. Fry until puffs are golden brown on the bottom; then turn and fry the other side.
5. Serve with yogurt and maple syrup, or apples stewed with cinnamon and honey, or Banana-Lemon Sauce (see p. 18).

Banana-Lemon Sauce

Serves 4
Total time: 10 minutes   **Penny**

This sauce is delicious with pancakes or French toast.

¼ **cup butter**
3 large bananas, diced
Juice of ½ lemon
Juice of 1 orange
Grated rind of 1 orange
1 tbsp. honey (or to taste)
2 tsp. cinnamon

1. In a small saucepan, melt butter. Add bananas.
2. Simmer until bananas are soft. Add remaining ingredients and serve hot.

Orange French Toast

Serves 6 to 8
Total time: 30 minutes   **Rico**

I think pancakes are too heavy. This is a tangy alternative.

4 eggs
½ **cup milk**
Juice of 1 orange
1 tbsp. grated orange rind
½ **tsp. cinnamon**
Sliced bread (whole-wheat or rye)
Butter or oil for frying

1. In a large bowl, mix together eggs, milk, orange juice, orange rind, and cinnamon.
2. Soak the bread in the egg mixture.

3. In a pan, melt butter or heat oil. Fry soaked bread, turning when crisp; fry the other side.
4. Serve with Banana-Lemon Sauce (see p. 18).

Note: It's important to soak the bread thoroughly so it isn't dry in the middle.

Breakfast Brown-Rice Muffins ✗✗

Makes 12 muffins
Total time: 30 minutes **Patsy**

Sometimes if I'm out of bread, I'll mix all the dry ingredients with the leftover brown rice at night and whip up the wet stuff in the morning. That way I can have muffins in almost the time it takes to bake them. By the time the kettle is boiled and the cat has been fed, the muffins are ready.

1 cup whole-wheat flour
¼ cup wheat germ
¼ cup bran
3 tsp. baking powder
½ tsp. salt
2 eggs, beaten
2 tbsp. brown sugar
¾ cup milk
¼ cup oil
⅔ cup cooked brown rice
½ cup raisins (optional)

1. In a very large bowl, mix together flour, wheat germ, bran, baking powder, and salt.
2. In another bowl, combine eggs, sugar, milk, and oil.
3. Add the egg mixture to the flour; add the rice and raisins. Stir until the dry ingredients are barely moistened.
4. Spoon into 12 well-greased muffin tins.
5. Bake in a 375 F oven for about 20 minutes.

Cranberry Delightful Muffins

Makes 12 muffins
Total time: 40 minutes **Patsy**

Good for breakfast yet not too sweet for "elevenses," these muffins are one of my favourites at tea-time. (Afternoon tea is a habit I picked up in England.)

- 1½ **cups whole-wheat flour**
- ¼ **cup bran**
- ¼ **cup wheat germ**
- 3 **tsp. baking powder**
- 2 **tsp. orange zest or grated orange rind (not the white part)**
- 1 **cup cranberries**
- 3 **tbsp. vegetable oil**
- 3 **tbsp. sugar**
- ½ **tsp. salt**
- 1 **cup milk**
- 1 **egg**

1. Mix together flour, bran, wheat germ, and baking powder.
2. Place zest or rind in a blender or a food processor. Add cranberries. Blend briefly. Then add oil, sugar, salt, milk, and egg, and blend until quite smooth.
3. Add mixture from blender or food processor to sifted dry ingredients. Stir until just moist.
4. Spoon into 12 well-greased muffin tins.
5. Bake in a 400 F oven for 20 minutes.

Note: Half a cup of walnuts or pecans can be added to dry ingredients.

Ginger Carob-Chip Muffins

Makes 12 muffins
Total time: 55 minutes   **Patsy**

Six years ago, I took these to Penny and John's cottage in Muskoka, and Penny's been trying to get the recipe ever since. Here it is.

1 cup 7-grain cereal
1 cup buttermilk
1 tsp. salt
¼ cup vegetable oil
3 tbsp. brown sugar
1 cup whole-wheat flour
1 tsp. baking powder
½ tsp. baking soda
½ tsp. cinnamon
1 tbsp. fresh grated ginger
1 cup carob chips

1. Place cereal in a mixing bowl. Add buttermilk, salt, oil, and sugar. Let batter stand half an hour. (If you plan to make muffins for breakfast, let the batter stand overnight.)
2. Sift together flour, baking powder, baking soda, and cinnamon. Add flour mixture to buttermilk mixture. Add grated ginger and carob chips. Stir until just moist. Add more buttermilk if mixture is too dry.
3. Spoon into 12 well-greased muffin tins.
4. Bake in a 375 F oven for 20 minutes.

Note: Because of the grain, these muffins have a chewy texture.

Penny's Granola

Makes 7 to 8 cups
Total time: 30 minutes   **Penny**

This recipe is the result of several years of experimenting. Served with yogurt and fresh fruit, it always gets rave reviews.

2 cups rolled oats
½ cup wheat flakes
½ cup bran
½ cup wheat germ
1 cup shredded dried, unsweetened coconut
1 cup chopped nuts (almonds, cashews, peanuts)
1 tsp. salt
½ cup raw sunflower seeds
⅓ cup vegetable or safflower oil
3 tbsp. honey
1 cup raisins
1 cup sesame seeds

1. In a large mixing bowl, combine oats, wheat flakes, bran, wheat germ, coconut, nuts, sunflower seeds, and salt.
2. In a large, heavy wok (preferably cast iron), heat oil and honey. Add cereal mixture and stir with wooden spoon over low heat until all ingredients are slightly moistened. If mixture is too dry, add a little more oil.
3. Turn up the flame and continue to stir. Toast until cereal is golden brown and crunchy. When granola is almost done, add raisins and heat until raisins are puffy. Remove from heat.
4. In a small wok, toast sesame seeds until golden brown. In a food processor, partially grind the seeds; about half the seeds should remain whole. Add to granola mix.
5. When granola is cool, store in closed jars or in a cookie tin. Granola is best served fresh, but will keep its crunchiness for about a week.

Note: If you prefer, you can spread the granola on cookie sheets to cook. Place granola under the broiler, stirring occasionally, until golden brown. Again, add sesame seeds after granola is cooked.

Shirred Eggs

Serves 8
Total time: 20 minutes   **Pamela**

No matter how much of this you make, there never seems to be enough: more people keep getting up for breakfast. I've taken to making the topping and letting people make their own eggs. For a more formal breakfast, I make a lot at once.

> **8 eggs**
> **1½ cups breadcrumbs**
> **½ tsp. dill weed**
> **½ tsp. chopped chives**
> **1 tbsp. chopped parsley (fresh or dried)**
> **¼ cup melted butter**
> **Salt and pepper to taste**

1. Grease 8 ramekins or muffin tins.
2. Break an egg into each ramekin or muffin tin.
3. In a mixing bowl, stir together the breadcrumbs, dill weed, chives, and parsley. Add butter. Toss. The mixture should not be soggy.
4. Spoon the breadcrumb topping over the eggs.
5. Bake in a 350 F oven for about 10 minutes. This is tricky, since every dish conducts heat differently. Muffin tins cook faster, but sometimes the eggs in the centre cook more slowly than the eggs around the outside. Soft eggs will jiggle slightly when shaken in the oven. Hard eggs start to puff up. If you are serving enough people, they want a variation anyway. Remember, the eggs continue to cook a little after you take them out of the oven.

Puffed Eggs Elora

Serves 1
Total time: 5 minutes **Elora**

Elora insists, "Don't put any little green things in my eggs."

> 2 eggs
> 4 drops milk
> 1 tsp. butter

1. Get a small bowl. Crack eggs into it. Stir with a fork. Add the milk and stir again.
2. In a small pan, melt the butter. Add the eggs and stir, over low heat, until cooked, about 3 minutes.

Banana-Yogurt Wake-Up Shake

Makes 3 cups
Total time: 5 minutes **Penny**

When you don't have time to cook breakfast, here's something quick and nutritious to start your day.

> 2 cups yogurt
> 1 cup water
> ½ cup apple juice or orange juice
> 1 banana
> 1 tsp. cinnamon
> 2 tbsp. lemon juice
> 1 tbsp. debittered brewer's yeast (optional)

1. Place all ingredients in blender and mix until frothy. If desired, add ice cubes and blend further.
Note: During strawberry season, throw in a few ripe berries for added zest and colour.

BRUNCHES/LUNCHES

Boxing Day Hangover Brunch

*Banana-Yogurt Wake-Up Shake *by Penny*

*Cranberry Delightful Muffins *by Patsy*

***Boxing Day Croquettes** by Pierre*

Coffee

Boxing Day Croquettes

Serves 4
Total time: 30 minutes **Pierre**

This solves the leftover-turkey-and-mashed-potato problem that faces everyone the morning after Christmas. It makes a great Boxing Day breakfast!

> **2 cups turkey meat**
> **2 cups mashed potatoes**
> **Salt to taste**
> **Olive or corn oil**
> **Dry mustard**

1. Chop the turkey meat or mince in a food processor. Blend with mashed potatoes and salt. Form into flat cakes. Pat mustard on one side.
2. In a skillet, heat oil. Place croquettes in skillet mustard-side down. Pat mustard on other side. Turn once. Serve when crisp.

Heavenly Corned-Beef Hash

serves 4
Total time: 20 minutes **Pierre**

This breakfast dish is for those who are hungry or those who have hangovers. It can be served with a poached egg on top for a family Sunday brunch.

> **1 10-ounce can corned beef**
> **1 large potato, finely chopped**
> **1 large onion, finely chopped**
> **1 egg**
> **1 tsp. black pepper**
> **2 tsp. celery salt**
> **2 tbsp. chopped parsley**

2 tbsp. red wine
2 tbsp. pancake flour
2 tbsp. dry English mustard
Oil for frying

1. Crumble the corned beef into a bowl. Add potato and onion. Mix.
2. Add egg and mix again.
3. Add pepper, celery salt, parsley, and wine. Mix, then sift in flour.
4. Mould mixture into flat patties. Sprinkle dry mustard on patties.
5. In an iron skillet, heat enough oil to prevent burning. Fry patties on both sides until crisp.

Harry's Welsh Rarebit

Serves 4
Total time: 20 minutes **Janet**

Pierre's best friend, the late Harry Filion, invented this variation on a famous savoury. He used to serve it for breakfast when he and his wife, Veryl (see her recipe for curried eggs on page 29) spent the Christmas holiday season with us. We think it's the best rarebit going.

1½ cups grated Cheddar cheese
1½ cups milk
1 egg
1 tsp. dry mustard
1 tbsp. cornstarch
1 tsp. Worcestershire sauce
1 tsp. salt
1 tsp. paprika

1. In the top of a double boiler, combine all ingredients. Blend well.
2. Cook over hot water until thick. Serve on toast.

Nasi Goreng Special (Fried Rice) ✕✕

Serves 4 to 6
Total time: 15 minutes

Penny and John

Even the tiniest food stalls in Indonesia serve this standby, but it's different in each town. This is our own version, and the one we like best. It's great if you're in a hurry; it's also a good way to use up leftovers. Make sure the rice is cool before you fry it.

¼ cup vegetable or sesame oil
2 to 3 large cloves of garlic, minced
1 tbsp. ginger, peeled and grated
1 large onion, chopped
1 or 2 chilies, or ½ tsp. cayenne
⅓ cup sesame seeds
⅓ cup peanuts (optional)
½ head cabbage, coarsely grated
2 carrots, chopped
½ cup chopped green beans, steamed
1 lb. fresh or frozen shrimp, shelled and
    dried (optional)
4 to 5 cups cooked brown rice, cooled
Salt to taste
Sliced tomato for garnish
Sliced cucumber for garnish
Tamari soy sauce to taste

1. In a large wok, heat oil. Sauté garlic, ginger, and onions until onions are transparent. Stir in chili or cayenne and cook for 1 minute.
2. Add sesame seeds and peanuts and fry quickly, over medium heat, stirring constantly.
3. When sesame seeds begin to brown, immediately add cabbage, carrots, beans, and shrimp (or other leftover vegetables or meat), and keep stirring until all ingredients are well coated with the oil mixture.
4. Add rice and salt and mix well.
5. Serve immediately. Garnish with sliced tomato and cucumber and sprinkle liberally with soy sauce.

Note: We often serve this for breakfast in Bali. To make the preparation quicker we leave out some or all of the vegetables and shrimp and serve with a gently fried egg on top.

Veryl's Curried Eggs

Serves 2
Total time: 15 minutes **Pierre**

When my friend Harry Filion and I were in the army together, his wife, Veryl, used to feed us these eggs on a Saturday night. We loved the eggs but we always claimed they weren't hot enough. Even though she kept increasing the amount of the curry we still complained. Veryl finally stopped making them, but not before I stole the recipe. Keep in mind that the hotter the curry, the more the dish calls for a cold lager.

White Sauce:
    2 tbsp. butter
    2 tbsp. all-purpose flour
    1 cup milk

    1 to 2 tbsp. Madras curry (or to taste)
    2 cups hot cooked rice
    6 eggs, poached

1. To make white sauce: In a small saucepan, melt butter to foaming. Stir in flour. Remove from heat. Stir in milk slowly. Return to heat. Bring to a boil, stirring constantly. Simmer for about 3 minutes.
2. Add curry to white sauce. Taste to ensure sauce is sufficiently piquant.
3. Place a cup of hot rice on each of two plates. Spoon 3 eggs on each plate.
4. Pour the curry sauce over the eggs. Serve.

Cheese Broccoli Bake

Serves 4
Total time: 40 minutes   **Penny**

Very few people are brave enough (or crazy enough) to invite
the entire Berton family to dinner. Once, ten years ago, when
I entertained our family en masse for Sunday brunch, I served
this dish. Since then, while I've been in Asia, it has become a
family favourite. Here's a slightly updated version.

> **Small bunch of broccoli, cut up in pieces**
> **5 or 6 cauliflowerets**
> **2 tbsp. butter**
> **1 clove garlic, minced**
> **1 large onion, chopped**
> **1 cup mushrooms, sliced**
> **1 tsp. cumin powder**
> **4 eggs, beaten**
> **2 cups cheese, grated (Cheddar, Gruyère, or**
> **Jarlsberg)**
> **½ tsp. nutmeg**
> **Salt and pepper to taste**

1. Steam broccoli and cauliflower until tender but firm
   (broccoli should still be a bright green colour). Arrange in
   a 2-quart greased casserole dish.
2. In a small skillet, heat butter. Sauté garlic and onion until
   onion is transparent. Add mushrooms and sauté. Stir in
   cumin and cook over low heat for 3 minutes, stirring
   constantly.
3. In a bowl, combine eggs and cheese. Add nutmeg, salt, and
   pepper. Add cooked onion mixture.
4. Pour mixture over vegetables in casserole. Bake in a 375 F
   oven for 20 minutes.
5. Serve immediately. Good with hot noodles or rice and a
   crisp green salad.
Note: Zucchini, sliced and steamed, makes a delicious
   alternative to the broccoli and cauliflower. If you use a
   salty cheese, you do not need to add any more salt to this
   dish.

Winter Pasta

Serves 2
Total time: 30 minutes **Peggy Anne**

This pasta dish is one of my favourites because I don't have to spend a lot of time making it or cleaning up afterwards.

½ pound bacon, diced
1 tbsp. garlic, minced
½ cup green onion, chopped
8 olives
2 eggs, beaten
Freshly ground black pepper
1 cup Parmesan cheese, grated
Fettuccine noodles for two

1. In a frying pan, fry bacon with garlic and ¼ cup of the green onion. When bacon is cooked but not crispy, add the olives.
2. Meanwhile, put a large pot of water with a pinch of salt on to boil.
3. In a bowl, combine eggs, remaining ¼ cup green onion and lots of freshly ground pepper. Stir in Parmesan cheese.
4. Drop fettuccine noodles into boiling water and cook according to package directions. When cooked, drain the noodles but don't rinse them.
5. Drain bacon mixture and add to egg mixture. Place egg and bacon in the pot pasta was cooked in; add pasta and mix well. The egg mixture cooks in the pasta, and the dish is ready to eat right away.

John Kline's Pie

Serves 4 to 6
Total time: 1 hour and 15 minutes   **Janet**

I developed this pie for the Doctor's House Restaurant in Kleinburg as a Canadian variation on the traditional Quiche Lorraine. We think it has more flavour and body than the original.

½ pound side bacon, thinly sliced
⅓ cup chopped green onions
3 eggs
2½ cups milk or cream
½ tsp. salt
¼ tsp. white pepper
Pinch dry English mustard
Pinch cayenne pepper
Freshly grated nutmeg
Chopped chives or parsley
Rich pastry for two 9-inch pie shells (see p. 186)
1½ cups grated old Canadian Cheddar

1. In a large skillet, fry bacon until it is really crisp. Remove bacon from skillet; drain and crumble; set aside.
2. In the same skillet, in the bacon grease, cook onions until soft. Drain and set aside.
3. In a bowl, beat the eggs with the milk. Add salt, pepper, mustard, cayenne, nutmeg, and chives or parsley. Stir.
4. Line 2 9-inch pie plates with pastry. Sprinkle the crumbled bacon over the pastry. Add the cooked onions and the cheese, then pour in the egg-milk mixture.
5. Bake in a 375 F oven for 45 minutes, or until the custard is set and the top is a golden brown.

Note: Small wedges of this pie, served warm, make an excellent starter. Larger sections make a substantial lunch.

Ooty Eggs

Serves 4
Total time: 30 minutes   **Paul**

"Ooty" is what most people call Ootacamund, a small town in India's Nilgiri Hills and one of the only cool places in the country south of the Himalayas. In some of the seedier hotels, this dish, better known as "egg-curry rice," is often the only thing on the menu.

> 1 tbsp. butter
> 4 cooking onions, sliced into rings
> 2 stalks celery, diced
> 1 tbsp. all-purpose flour
> 2 cups chicken stock
> 1 cup wine or water or chicken broth
> 4 tbsp. curry
> 4 eggs, hard-boiled, peeled

1. In a medium-sized saucepan, melt butter. Sauté onion rings and celery.
2. When the mixture is soft, add flour and stir for 30 seconds.
3. Add the chicken stock, wine (or water or broth), and curry. Boil for 10 minutes.
4. Add the whole hard-boiled eggs. Serve immediately over rice with chutney or fruit as a condiment.

Procrastination Banana Bread

Makes 1 loaf
Total time: 1 hour and 30 minutes **Perri**

This banana bread tastes so good because I experimented with it over and over at university instead of writing essays and studying for exams. That's why we called it procrastination bread!

½ **cup butter**
¾ **cup sugar**
2 eggs
1 tsp. vanilla
3 bananas, mashed
1 to 2 tsp. lemon rind
2 cups all-purpose flour
2½ **tsp. baking powder**
½ **tsp. salt**
1 cup chopped walnuts

1. Cream butter and sugar.
2. Add eggs one at a time, beating after each addition.
3. Add vanilla, mashed bananas, and lemon rind.
4. Sift together flour, baking powder, and salt.
5. Add to banana mixture. Beat until mixed. Add nuts. Stir.
6. Put in a greased loaf tin. Bake in a 350 F oven for 1 hour or until a fork comes out clean.

Note: Sugar can be reduced to ½ cup if desired.

Johnnycake

Makes 1 8-inch square cake
Total time: 30 minutes

Pamela

Inspired by pioneer writer Catherine Parr Traill's recipe, this cake has been adapted for the campfire.

Dry ingredients:
 1 cup corn meal
 1 cup all-purpose or whole-wheat flour
 1 tsp. salt
 1 tsp. baking soda
 1 tsp. sugar
 ⅓ cup powdered milk
 1 tsp. powdered ginger

Wet ingredients:
 1 tbsp. vinegar
 ¼ cup vegetable oil
 1 cup water

1. Before you leave home, mix the dry ingredients together and store in a plastic bag.
2. At the campfire, when the coals have burned down, place the dry ingredients in a pan.
3. Mix the wet ingredients together, then add them to the dry ingredients. Stir quickly, just enough to moisten everything.
4. Wrap the pan in aluminum foil or place another pan on top, and cook for about 20 minutes over the coals. Try not to burn the bottom.
5. Serve with chili or beans, or for breakfast with butter and maple syrup.

Note: If you aren't a camper, you can make this in the oven. Bake in a 400 F oven for 20 minutes. If you use real milk, mix it with the vinegar to make sour milk before adding the oil.

Curried Squash/Pumpkin Soup �✕✕

Serves 6
Total time: 1 hour   **Penny**

I serve this for lunch with cornbread or muffins.

¼ **cup butter**
3 **large onions, chopped**
3 **cloves garlic, minced**
1 **tbsp. fresh ginger, finely grated**
1 **tbsp. curry powder**
1 **tsp. cumin powder**
½ **tsp. cayenne (or to taste)**
1 **tsp. Garam Masala (available at East Indian food**
    stores)
1 **large pumpkin or 2 or 3 small squash, boiled,**
    peeled, and mashed
1 **quart vegetable stock or water**

1. In a heavy, deep saucepan (I use a cast-iron wok), melt
   butter. Add onions, garlic, and ginger, and sauté until
   onion is transparent. Add curry powder, cumin powder,
   cayenne, and Garam Masala. Cook over low heat, stirring
   with a wooden spoon, for about 5 minutes.
2. Add pumpkin and stock or water. Bring to a boil, then
   lower heat and simmer for 30 minutes, stirring
   occasionally.
3. For a smooth soup, mix in blender.

DRINKS

Full Moon in May

*Kleinburg Julep by Pierre

*Persian Lemon Soup by Janet

*Asparagus Salad by Patsy

*Dandelion Salad by Pamela

*Shrimp and Snow Peas in Coconut Cream

by Penny

Rice by John

*Spring Rhubarb Pie by Perri

Kleinburg Julep

Serves 4 to 6
Total time: 10 minutes, or 1 hour and 10 minutes   **Pierre**

Since we have a lot of fresh mint growing along the river and beside the duck ponds, this is a popular if potent drink for a summer's afternoon – but only for those over nineteen.

> **2 handfuls of fresh mint leaves**
> **4 tbsp. sugar**
> **Juice of 3 lemons**
> **13 ounces rye or bourbon whiskey**
> **Soda water**
> **Mint leaves for garnish**

1. In a bowl, place the mint leaves and cover with sugar, lemon juice, and whiskey.
2. With a fork or the back of a spoon, bruise and crush the mint well.
3. Fill 4 or more metal cups with crushed ice. Add a short straw.
4. Place a portion of whiskey mixture in each cup. Fill with soda water and garnish with mint leaves.

Note: If you can bear to wait, chill the cups in the fridge or freezer for an hour before making the drinks.

Muskoka Sunrise

Serves 1
Total time: 5 minutes   **Peter**

Once, on a hot Sunday in Muskoka, we found ourselves short of tonic water and miles from a store. The pantry provided an agreeable substitute.

    2 ounces vodka
    3 ounces orange juice
    3 ounces cranberry juice
    1 slice lime

1. Fill a tall highball glass with ice. Pour vodka over ice.
2. Add orange juice.
3. Gently pour the cranberry juice down the edge of the glass and watch it slide past the orange juice to the bottom.
4. Garnish with lime slice.

Note: The orange and cranberry layers create a pleasing sunrise effect.

Bali Sunset

Serves 6
Total time: 10 minutes   **John**

People from around the world have gathered on our porch in Bali to sip this drink and watch the sun set over the rice fields.

    12 ounces rum
    ½ cup lemon juice
    Cinnamon to taste
    Sugar to taste
    4 bananas
    Chopped ice to chill

1. Place all ingredients in a blender. Blend until smooth.

Fruit Daiquiri

Serves 4
Total time: 20 minutes   **Peter**

We serve this all the time during the summer, when fruit is in season. It's a great summer drink for a small group.

¼ cup freshly squeezed lemon juice
5 tsp. sugar
Ice cubes
8 ounces dark rum
1 cup fresh raspberries or strawberries or 2 bananas,
**   or 2 large peaches, or whatever else you've got**
1 tsp. grated lemon peel

1. Place ¼ cup of the lemon juice in a shallow dish; place 1 tbsp. of the sugar in a separate shallow dish.
2. Rinse 4 stemmed glasses in water. Dip the rim of each glass in lemon juice, then dip in sugar. Immediately place the glasses in the freezer for at least 15 minutes.
3. Fill blender one-third full of ice cubes.
4. To the blender, add rum, remaining 2 tbsp. sugar, remaining ½ cup lemon juice, and fruit. Blend until smooth.
5. Pour into frosted glasses and sprinkle with grated lemon peel.

Note: The amount of sugar you use depends on what fruit is used. Strawberries, for example, are sweet in season but not in winter. Bananas will likely not require any sugar, and they often make a very good substitute for sugar when using a tart fruit.

Instant Hot Rum

Serves 6
Total time: 3 minutes   **Pierre**

Advance preparation allows you to make a hot rum quickly on a skiing trip or during a picnic. We used this recipe when the family went down the Yukon River. Alas, we forgot that some Yukon rum is 151-proof. Don't use Yukon rum – at least not before the tents go up.

½ **cup brown sugar**
½ **cup butter**
Juice of 3 lemons
½ **tsp. nutmeg**
½ **tsp. cinnamon**
½ **tsp. cloves**
12 ounces dark rum

1. Mix all ingredients except the rum together thoroughly and store in a jar.
2. When you need hot rum in a hurry, combine 2 ounces of rum and 2 tbsp. of the mixture in a cup, then fill with hot water.

Hot Ginger and Lemon

Serves 4
Total time: 5 minutes   **Penny**

This is my favourite drink during the rainy season in Bali —
especially when a cold or sore throat threatens. Ginger and
lemon have cleansing and healing properties. Even when you're
healthy, it's a delicious, refreshing drink.

2 tbsp. finely grated fresh ginger root
6 cups boiling water
Fresh lemon juice to taste
Honey to taste

1. Put ginger in a warmed teapot.
2. Pour boiling water over ginger; steep for 5 minutes; strain
   into cups.
3. To each cup, add lemon and honey to taste.
Note: When I have a cold, I fill a thermos with this and sip it
   all day.

APPETIZERS

Summer Solstice Barbecue

*Fruit Daiquiri *by Peter*

***Soy Beef** *by Pierre*

*Borscht on the Rocks *by Janet*

*Honey-Garlic Barbecued Chicken *by Paul*

*Dilled Carrot Salad *by Patsy*

*Saffron Sesame Rice *by John*

*Strawberry Dip *by Pamela*

Soy Beef

Serves 4 to 6
Total time: Overnight **Pierre**

You can make this in the winter if you have an open fireplace, or in the summer if you have a barbecue.

1 large onion, chopped
1 clove garlic, minced
2 cups soy sauce
1 pound filet or sirloin steak, cut in bite-sized pieces

1. In a bowl, combine onion, garlic, and soy sauce.
2. Add meat and marinate overnight.
3. Give your guests small skewers or fondue forks. Let them cook their marinated meat, a piece at a time, over the coals.

Drunken Mushrooms

Serves 10
Total time: 30 minutes **Pierre**

One day in 1964, Patsy's horse Prince left some souvenirs at the top of the hill beside our house. Next year we had a lovely crop of mushrooms – and ever since we've had scores of fat field mushrooms as a reminder of the horse (now deceased). That's how I developed this dish. But if you have no horse and no wild mushrooms, you can use the tame variety. They make a delicious hors d'oeuvre before a big dinner party.

½ cup butter
1 pound mushrooms, peeled (if necessary) and finely chopped
1 cup red wine
Salt and pepper to taste
20 small squares of buttered toast

1. In a skillet, melt the butter. Reduce heat. Add mushrooms, wine, salt, and pepper.
2. Cook, stirring occasionally, until mushrooms form a golden-brown mass.
4. Spread on squares of toast and serve.

Devilled Ham

Serves 8
Total time: 10 minutes　　　　　　　　　　　　　**Peter**

In Kleinburg, there is often leftover ham because my mother frequently serves it at parties. When leftovers are not available, canned ham suffices.

2 cups chopped ham
3 tbsp. Miracle Whip
2 tbsp. red pepper or diced pimento
Dash Worcestershire
½ small onion, chopped
1 tsp. dry mustard
Cracked pepper

1. Place all ingredients in food processor. Mix until they form a paste.
2. Serve on crackers or bread.
Note: For sandwiches, the mixture is best when it's coarser.

Chicken Pâté

A lot of people won't eat liver, but even those who can't stand the thought of it usually like this. Even Peter and John loved it.

> **2 tbsp. butter or chicken fat**
> **2 cloves garlic, minced**
> **1 onion, minced**
> **1 tbsp. grated ginger**
> **Dash coriander**
> **Dash curry powder**
> **Dash cinnamon**
> **Salt and pepper to taste**
> **1 pound chicken livers, chopped fine**
> **Lime or lemon juice to taste**
> **1 tsp. sherry**
> **2 tbsp. table cream**
> **2 hard-boiled eggs, chopped fine**

1. In a skillet, melt chicken fat or butter. Add garlic, onion, ginger, coriander, curry powder, cinnamon, and salt. Sauté. Add chicken liver and sauté until liver is cooked.
2. Add lime or lemon juice and sherry.
3. Place mixture in blender. Add cream and blend until creamy.
4. Stir in chopped egg.
5. Spread on crackers or toast to serve. Or store in a closed jar in the fridge.

Steak Tartare

Serves 40 – one piece each
Total time: 30 minutes **Pierre**

We've all been to parties where the meal, usually a buffet, is served very late in the evening because some guests are tardy and the host keeps pouring very stiff drinks and everybody is absolutely starving for something more substantial than potato chips to act as blotting paper. This is your answer. People will fall on it like a pack of ravenous wolves, as long as you do not reveal to them that they are eating raw meat. Tell them anything except that awful truth.

> **2 pounds sirloin steak, ground (have butcher grind it twice)**
> **2 egg yolks**
> **½ cup finely chopped onions**
> **1 tbsp. Worcestershire sauce**
> **1 tsp. dry English mustard**
> **1 tsp. salt**
> **Freshly ground pepper to taste**
> **Slices of French or rye bread (about 40)**
> **Capers for garnish**
> **Parsley for garnish**

1. In a bowl, mix meat, egg yolks, onions, Worcestershire sauce, mustard, salt, and pepper.
2. Spread the mixture liberally on bread (to the very edge, please) and garnish with capers and parsley.

Note: This is one of those recipes where personal tastes are important. When mixing, keep tasting; add more seasoning if you like it hot.

Peter's Crunchy Dill Pickles

Makes about 6 1-quart jars
Total time: 1 hour   **Peter**

This is a good dill-pickle recipe because it's quick. Once made,
the jars should be kept cool. The pickles can probably be eaten
within two weeks, but should be left no longer than four months
– eat them while they're still crunchy. Refrigerate before serving. Choose only cucumbers that have prickles to ensure fresh-
ness. The grape leaves apparently keep the pickles crunchy –
but if you can't find any, leave them out.

> **6 quarts cucumbers, each 3 to 4 inches long**
> **6 cloves garlic**
> **1 cup fresh dill (12 sprigs)**
> **6 grape leaves (optional)**
> **1 quart pickling vinegar**
> **¾ cup pickling salt**
> **2 quarts water**
> **½ cup pickling spice**

1. Soak cucumbers in cold water and scrub them with a
   brush to remove the prickles and dirt.
2. Pack pickles neatly into 6 sterilized 1-quart jars, fitting as
   many in as possible. Add one clove of garlic, 2 sprigs of
   whole dill (with seeds), and one grape leaf to each jar. Set
   aside.
3. Place vinegar, salt, water, and pickling spice in a pot and
   bring to a boil. Pour hot liquid into the packed jars to the
   brim. Allow to settle for 10 minutes or so, then fill the jars
   again.
4. Repeat this process as necessary. Seal the jars tightly and
   store in a cool place. (The refrigerator is best.)

Note: Every time I make this, I use different amounts of
things – that is, I always seem to run out of liquid or not
have enough cucumbers. If you need more liquid, simply
make up more in the same proportions.

Peter's Pickled Peppers (with Cucumbers)

Makes 6 quarts
Total time: 1 hour

Peter

Follow the previous recipe but use several fresh, hot, spicy peppers instead of a few of the cucumbers in each jar. It really improves the flavour of the pickles.

Chili Garlic Spaghetti

Serves 4
Total time: 20 minutes

Rico

In Indonesia, when we had time on our hands, we always served this using freshly made pasta.

½ **cup olive oil**
2 tbsp. minced garlic
4 tbsp. minced scallions
1 tbsp. fresh minced green chilies (no seeds)
Spaghetti or linguine for four

1. In a heavy wok (preferably cast iron), heat olive oil. Sauté garlic, scallions, and chilies over medium heat until soft.
2. Meanwhile, drop pasta into rapidly boiling salted water. Cook until tender to a fork (about 10 minutes for dried pasta, less for fresh). Drain pasta, rinse quickly in hot water, and add immediately to garlic mixture in wok.
3. Toss ingredients together until pasta is well-coated with garlic mixture. Serve immediately on heated plates.

Devilled Dungeness Crab

Serves 10
Total time: 15 minutes **Janet**

Devilled Crab is probably the first dish I ever made for which anyone requested the recipe. When we were first married and living in a one-room apartment in Vancouver, Scott Young, an editor at *Maclean's*, was sent out to Vancouver to scout Pierre, and possibly hire him for the magazine. Scott came for dinner and enjoyed the crab dish so much he called again and again from various parts of the country to ask for it. I guess I just sort of put it together, as I don't suppose I had many cookbooks at the time. Since then, however, I always order it if it's on a menu. This combination is still one of my favourites. (P.S. Pierre got the job!)

¼ **cup butter**
1 tbsp. finely chopped shallot
2 tbsp. finely chopped celery
1 tbsp. finely chopped green pepper
3 tbsp. all-purpose flour
1 cup milk or cream
Salt and pepper to taste
Dash Worcestershire sauce
Dash dry mustard
Dash cayenne pepper
2 cups fresh, frozen, or canned crab meat
Grated cheese
Butter for broiling

1. In a saucepan, melt butter. Sauté shallot, celery, and green pepper until soft, but not brown.
2. Stir in flour and cook for a few minutes. Add milk or cream, stirring constantly. Stir in salt, pepper, Worcestershire sauce, mustard, and cayenne.
3. Carefully fold in crab meat. Add more milk if mixture is too dry.

4. Pour the mixture into buttered scallop shells or a large au gratin dish. Sprinkle with grated cheese and dot with butter.
5. Place casserole under the broiler for a few minutes until the mixture bubbles. Serve at once.

Note: Chopped hard-boiled eggs or a drop of sherry may be added for variety. This dish serves 5 as a main course.

Spicy Crab Snacks

Serves 8
Total time: 15 minutes **Peter**

It's always best not to leave the room when this is served. There is a good chance there will be none left when you return!

1 6-ounce can crab meat
1½ heaping tbsp. Miracle Whip
Juice of ½ lemon
2 tsp. curry powder
2 tsp. chopped chives
½ tsp. dry mustard
Cracked pepper to taste
8 slices toast, cut into quarters

1. Place all ingredients except the toast in a bowl. Mix with a fork until smooth.
2. Spread on toast and serve.

Note: If made in a food processor, this comes out as pâté. Use only 1 tbsp. Miracle Whip. You could also add finely chopped shallot and celery for crunch.

Ceviche

Serves 6
Total time: 4 hours and 20 minutes   **Pamela**

We first had this appetizer on a family holiday in Acapulco after we caught a bonito in the Pacific. Even without fresh bonito, in a cold Canadian winter, it still brings back memories of the view–skimming pelicans in the last flash of sunset.

1 pound very fresh, firm fish (sole, snapper, or scallops), cut into bite-sized pieces
½ cup diced Spanish onion
10 cherry tomatoes, quartered and seeded
¼ cup diced green pepper
¼ cup diced red sweet pepper
¼ cup chopped fresh parsley

Marinade:
1 cup fresh lime juice (about 8 limes)
½ cup water
3 garlic cloves, crushed
½ tsp. dry hot mustard
Freshly ground pepper
¼ tsp. Tabasco sauce
2 tbsp. olive oil

1. Place fish, onions, tomatoes, peppers, and parsley in a deep glass or ceramic bowl.
2. Place all marinade ingredients except olive oil in a jar with a tight-fitting lid. Shake well. Add olive oil. Shake again.
3. Pour marinade over fish, making sure the marinade covers the fish completely.
4. Marinate for at least 4 hours in the refrigerator. The lime juice "cooks" the fish, and it will have a texture somewhat like chicken.

Note: Don't use bottled lime juice–it doesn't work.

Spiral Rigatoni with Shrimp and Ginger

✕ ✕

Serves 4 as an appetizer
Total time: 30 minutes

Patsy

I had a dish similar to this once in an Italian restaurant. I rushed home and tried to make it. The result was a delectable facsimile!

1 500-g. package spiral rigatoni
4 to 5 tbsp. olive oil
3 garlic cloves, minced
3 to 4 shallots, minced
1 tbsp. fresh ginger, chopped fine
¼ tsp. fresh green chili (optional)
½ cup red pepper, sliced as thin as possible
½ cup green pepper, sliced as thin as possible
1 pound shrimp, peeled and washed
1 tbsp. chicken stock (if moisture is needed)
½ tsp. Tamari soy sauce
Salt and pepper to taste

1. Cook rigatoni al dente, 7 to 10 minutes, or according to package directions.
2. In a large skillet, heat oil. Sauté garlic, shallots, and ginger for 5 minutes, or until shallots are soft and transparent.
3. Add chili, peppers, and shrimp. Sauté until shrimp just loses transparency, about 3 to 4 minutes. Add stock, if necessary, and soy sauce.
4. Add rigatoni. Toss and heat. Season with salt and pepper to taste.

Spicy Squidbits

Serves 4 to 12
Total time: 30 minutes **John**

This tasty treat gets eaten faster than you can fry it.

> **4 pounds squid, pre-cleaned**
> **½ cup all-purpose flour**
> **1 tbsp. curry powder**
> **½ tsp. cayenne (or to taste)**
> **1 cup sesame seeds**
> **Salt and pepper to taste**
> **Peanut or safflower oil for frying**
> **Fresh lemon juice**

1. Slice squid crosswise into quarter-inch rings.
2. Place flour, curry powder, cayenne, sesame seeds, salt, and pepper in a plastic bag. Shake to mix.
3. Place slices of squid, a few at a time, in the bag of flour. Shake to coat.
4. In a deep fryer, fry squid slices in hot oil until squid is brown. Serve immediately with a squeeze of lemon.

Note: If you buy less than 4 pounds of squid, you'll be sorry.

Hibachi Oysters

Serves 6
Total time: 30 minutes **Peter**

This is a good outdoor appetizer because in the summer oysters are better cooked than raw. We first had them in 1975 on Galiano Island, where we could pick oysters off the beach.

> **36 large oysters**
> **½ cup butter**
> **3 lemons**

1. Shuck oysters and cut meat away from shell.
2. Place 8 to 10 oysters, in their shells, on a hibachi or over a low fire.
3. Add 1 tsp. butter to each oyster and squeeze in lemon until shell is filled to brim.
4. When butter is foaming, remove oyster meat from the shell with a small fork. Eat immediately.
5. Leave shells over fire and re-use. It's easier to use the same shells for cooking because they're hot. When a shell turns black, discard it and begin another.

Deep-Fried Smelts

Serves 4 to 12
Total time: 30 minutes **John**

These are delectable nibbles that happen only once a year. Enjoy them while you can!

4 pounds smelts
½ cup all-purpose flour
1 tbsp. curry powder
½ tsp. cayenne (or to taste)
1 cup sesame seeds
Salt and pepper to taste
Peanut or safflower oil
Fresh lemon juice

1. Dry smelts with paper towels.
2. Place flour, curry powder, cayenne, sesame seeds, salt, and pepper in a paper bag. Add smelts and shake to coat.
3. In a deep fryer, fry smelts in hot oil until brown.
4. Serve immediately, with a squeeze of lemon.

Trendy Potato Skins

Serves 4
Total time: 1 hour

Perri

I used to eat these in "hot spots" and trendy restaurants, but they were always greasy and often cold. So I started making my own.

> 4 potatoes
> 4 pieces of bacon
> ¼ cup melted butter
> 1 cup grated Cheddar cheese
> 1 tomato, diced
> 1 green pepper, diced
> 1 onion, chopped (optional)
> Sour cream for garnish
> Dill for garnish

1. Wash potatoes and bake in a 375 F oven for 50 minutes or until cooked.
2. Fry bacon until crisp. Drain and crumble.
3. Cut potatoes in half and scoop out the insides, being careful not to pierce the skins.
4. Drench potato skins in melted butter, inside and out.
5. Place skins under broiler for 2 to 3 minutes. Watch carefully to make sure they don't burn.
6. Remove skins from oven. Place a little grated cheese inside each one. Sprinkle with bacon, tomatoes, green peppers, and onions. Top with more grated cheese.
7. Place under broiler for 3 to 5 minutes. Again, be careful not to let them burn.
8. Serve immediately with sour cream and dill.

Note: Save the inside of the potatoes for Shepherd's Pie (see p. 138).

SOUPS

MENU

Winter Supper

*Drunken Mushrooms *by Pierre*

*Janet's Soup *by Janet*

*Chicken and Oyster Pie *by Janet*

Rice *by John*

*Green Salad with Tangy Tomato Salad Dressing

by Eric

*Better Broccoli *by Penny*

*Zabaglione *by Pamela*

Janet's Soup

Serves 10
Total time: Several days **Janet**

This soup, which appeared in Pierre and Janet Berton's Canadian Food Guide, is now legendary. People still stop me on the street to discuss the recipe.

1 large beef heart
8 quarts cold water
4 stalks celery, chopped
3 large onions, chopped
2 carrots, chopped
½ turnip, diced
¼ green pepper, chopped
2 28-ounce cans tomatoes
½ tsp. summer savory
¼ cup fresh parsley, chopped
½ cup fresh chives
1 tsp. basil
1 tsp. dry English mustard
Dash Worcestershire sauce
Dash Angostura bitters
Salt and pepper to taste
1 tsp. celery seed

1. In a large soup pot, place beef heart and 4 quarts of the cold water. Bring to a boil and skim. Simmer over low heat for several hours or until juice tastes like your great grandmother's old-fashioned beef tea. Alternatively, cook in a pressure cooker for 30 minutes. Remove the heart and reserve.
2. To the broth, add celery, onions, carrots, turnip, and green pepper. Simmer for about half an hour or until vegetables are just crunchy.
3. Add tomatoes, savory, parsley, chives, basil, mustard, Worcestershire sauce, Angostura bitters, salt and pepper, and celery seed. Simmer for another 10 minutes. Serve.
4. For the next day, put the beef heart in remaining 4 quarts of water, bring to a boil and simmer. (Old cookbooks say

the soup pot should "smile, not laugh.") This process can be repeated for days and days. It is surprising how much flavour still remains in the soup stock. If there are some old vegetables left from a previous cooking (yesterday's green beans, for example, will have turned grey in the soup), place them in the blender with a little fresh stock; blend and return to pot. Put a fresh batch of vegetables in the soup. Use anything you happen to have on hand. Turnip gives a bit of a nip, while carrots make the soup sweet.

The soup improves with age. As it simmers on the back of the stove, the water in which other vegetables have been cooked may be added to it. If the stock becomes too thick, simply strain and start again.

And don't throw out that beef heart. It can be converted to Shepherd's Pie (see p. 138) or stuffed with breadcrumbs, onions, and celery mixed with summer savory, parsley, chives, mustard, Worcestershire sauce, and bitters. Bake in a 325 F oven for half an hour and serve as a main dish with baked potatoes.

Persian Lemon Soup

Serves 4 to 6
Total time: 30 minutes **Janet**

There's nothing like a light, refreshing soup to start off a hearty meal, but who wants another bowl of consommé? This soup, developed from an old Persian recipe, is the answer.

> **6 cups chicken stock**
> **1 tsp. celery seed**
> **⅓ cup uncooked white rice**
> **3 eggs, beaten well**
> **Juice of 2 lemons**
> **1 tbsp. cold water**
> **Salt and pepper to taste**

1. Bring chicken stock to a boil. Add celery seed.
2. Wash the rice and add it to the stock. Cook till rice is soft.
3. In a bowl, combine eggs, lemon juice, and water.
4. Take a little stock and pour it slowly over the egg mixture, stirring all the time. Pour a little more stock into the egg mixture, then pour egg and stock back into the saucepan. Add salt and pepper. Stir well.
5. Serve at once. Or chill and serve cold.

Note: Don't boil the soup after you've added the eggs and lemon juice or it will curdle.

Borscht on the Rocks

Serves 4 to 6
Total time: 3 hours **Janet**

This light summer soup makes a colourful start to a meal. We once served it to the late Alfred Knopf, the famous New York publisher, who was renowned as a gourmet. He liked it.

> **3 cups peeled, chopped beets (about 6 beets)**
> **1 quart soup stock (made from beef soup bones)**
> **2 onions, chopped**
> **1 cup chopped cabbage**

Salt and pepper to taste
1 tsp. celery salt
1 tbsp. lemon juice
Dairy sour cream or yogurt for topping

1. In a large soup pot, put beets, soup stock, onions, and cabbage. (Reserve one beet for use later.)
2. Simmer over medium heat until vegetables are tender. Strain the mixture and add salt and pepper, celery salt, and lemon juice to the liquid. Grate in one raw beet for colour. Chill for 2 hours.
3. Serve over ice cubes in very tall glasses. Top with sour cream or yogurt. Drink through a straw.

Note: The whole mixture may be put through the blender and served in bowls as a thick soup.

Chilled Cucumber Soup ✗

Serves 10
Total time: 15 minutes and 2 hours to chill   **Pamela**

A great soup when the garden is in full bloom and it's too hot to cook.

1 Spanish onion, peeled and quartered
Juice of 2 fresh limes
2 cucumbers, peeled, cut lengthwise, and seeded
2½ cups buttermilk
1 cup sour cream
1 tbsp. chopped fresh dill weed
1 tbsp. chopped fresh chives

1. Place the onion in a blender with the lime juice. Blend.
2. Add one of the cucumbers and some of the buttermilk; blend.
3. Pour the blended mixture into a jug (most blenders are too small to blend the soup in one batch) and blend the other cucumber and remaining buttermilk in batches.
4. To the last batch, add the sour cream and blend again briefly. Stir all the batches together in a bowl or jug.
5. Chill for at least 2 hours. Serve garnished with dill and chives.

Summertime Soup

Serves 6
Total time: 45 minutes   **Pierre**

Make this soup from the harvest from your own garden or from the stuff sold at country roadside stands any August day. Pamela runs the Berton garden and we all make the soup.

> **6 quarts fresh tomatoes, cut in quarters**
> **1 cup water**
> **1 bunch celery, chopped (leaves and all)**
> **20 fresh green onions, chopped**
> **1 large cooking onion, chopped**
> **2 cloves garlic**
> **2 tbsp. basil**
> **1 tsp. oregano**
> **Salt**
> **Cayenne to taste**
> **Worcestershire sauce to taste**

1. Place the tomatoes in a large pot with water. Simmer.
2. Add celery and onions. Simmer for 30 minutes.
3. Add garlic, basil, oregano, salt, cayenne, and Worcestershire sauce. Stir well. Serve hot or cold.

Variations:

Tomato Purée
> After cooking, mash the soup with a potato masher or put in blender. For a clear soup, strain liquid through a sieve.

Cream Summer Soup
> Stir Tomato Purée into a white sauce (see p. 29), heat, and serve.

Apple-Curry Soup

Serves 4 to 6
Total time: 1 hour   **Penny**

This tangy soup livens up ordinary chicken stock.

¼ cup butter
2 large onions, chopped
2 cloves garlic, minced
1 tbsp. ginger, finely grated
2 small apples, peeled and diced
1 tbsp. curry powder
½ tsp. cayenne (optional)
Salt to taste
4 cups chicken stock
Juice of 1 lemon (optional)
1 cup table cream (optional)
1 lemon, sliced

1. In a large, heavy saucepan or a cast-iron wok, melt butter. Sauté onions, garlic, and ginger until onions are soft.
2. Add apples, curry powder, cayenne, and salt, and continue to cook over low heat, stirring constantly, until apples are soft.
3. Add chicken stock and bring to a boil.
4. Place hot mixture in a blender and blend until smooth.
5. Return to saucepan and simmer for 20 minutes, adding water if soup becomes too thick.
6. When ready to serve, add lemon juice to taste. If desired, add cream as well, stirring with a wire whisk to prevent curdling.
7. To serve, ladle into bowls and float a slice of lemon in each bowl.

Note: You may add leftover chicken to the soup, as well; add with the stock.

Jerusalem Root Soup

Serves 6
Total time: 1 hour and 30 minutes   **Patsy**

This vegetable soup has a unique sweet taste. I used to make it in England, where it is easier to find Jerusalem artichokes. Here they seem to be available for only a couple of weeks each fall.

  3 tbsp. vegetable oil
  2 onions, chopped
  2 cloves garlic, crushed
  2 carrots, chopped
  3 celery stalks, chopped
  ½ cabbage, chopped
  5 or 6 medium-sized Jerusalem artichokes, chopped
  Dried basil to taste
  Dried savory to taste
  2 bay leaves
  Salt and pepper to taste
  4 cups water
  2 to 3 tbsp. lemon juice
  Yogurt for garnish (optional)

1. In a large saucepan, heat oil. Sauté onions and garlic until onions are transparent.
2. Add carrots, celery, cabbage, artichokes, basil, savory, bay leaves, salt, and pepper. Add water and bring to a boil. Simmer for 35 minutes.
3. Place soup in blender. Blend until smooth. Add lemon juice.
4. Serve with a dollop of yogurt if you like.

Tom Kha Gai (Thai Coconut-Chicken Soup)

Serves 10
Total time: 30 minutes   **Pamela**

I worked with a group that developed Toronto's first Thai restaurant, Bangkok Garden. We served this rich, piquant soup for a series of promotional lunches. It is still my favourite, and I make it for special dinners. Once you have found the exotic ingredients in your local Oriental supermarket, the soup is easy to make.

> 3 10-ounce cans coconut cream
> ½ cup dried kha (Alpinia galanga or galingale)
> 4 Kaffir lime leaves
> 2 stalks lemon grass
> 3 whole chicken breasts, boned and cut into half-inch pieces
> ½ cup lemon juice
> 3 tbsp. fish sauce
> 1 tbsp. chopped fresh coriander leaves
> 1 tbsp. tiny hot fresh chilies

1. In a large soup pot, combine coconut cream, kha, lime leaves, and lemon grass. Bring to a boil and simmer for 5 minutes.
2. Add chicken and simmer for 15 minutes.
3. Remove from heat. Add lemon juice and fish sauce.
4. Garnish with coriander and chilies and serve hot.

Note: The kha is not eaten, and the faint-hearted should be warned about the chilies.

Borscht Vegetarian

Serves 6
Total time: 1 hour and 30 minutes   **Patsy**

In our house we usually had blended borsch. I never knew what was in it until I had this kind of borscht at my Aunt Lucy's. I remember the way she cut the beets in long strips. It makes a hearty meal with black bread and cheese.

2 to 4 large beets
3 to 4 tbsp. butter
2 large onions, chopped
3 cloves garlic, pressed
2 carrots, chopped
½ cabbage, shredded
1 28-ounce can tomatoes
2 bay leaves
1 tsp. oregano
1 tsp. savory
1 tsp. thyme
1 tsp. basil
1 tsp. caraway seeds or dill seeds
2 to 3 tbsp. lemon juice
Salt and pepper to taste
1 small raw beet

1. In a covered saucepan, cook large beets in boiling water for 45 minutes. Drain. Peel beets and cut neatly into long strips.
2. In a heavy, large saucepan, melt butter. Sauté onions until clear.
3. Add garlic and carrots and stir. Cook over medium heat for 10 minutes. Add shredded cabbage and cook for another 10 minutes.
4. Add tomatoes, cooked beets, bay leaves, oregano, savory, thyme, basil, caraway seeds, lemon juice, salt, and pepper. Simmer for at least 30 minutes.
5. Before serving, grate the small raw beet into the soup to add colour.

Note: This soup is even better the next day – or the next.

Corny Soup

Serves 4 to 6
Total time: 30 minutes **Pierre and Penny**

During the corn season, we always have a lot of extra ears of corn that have been cooked but not eaten. We use them up in Corny Soup.

> 2 tbsp. butter
> 1 clove garlic, minced (optional)
> 1 onion, chopped
> 1 tbsp. all-purpose flour
> 2 cups milk
> 2 cups corn (fresh, canned, or frozen)
> Salt and black pepper to taste
> Nutmeg to taste
> Dash Tamari soy sauce
> Dash cayenne
> 1 tbsp. lemon juice
> Fresh parsley or dill, chopped fine, for garnish

1. In a heavy saucepan, melt butter. Sauté garlic and onion until onion is transparent.
2. Add flour and stir with a wooden spoon for 3 minutes.
3. Turn heat to low. Gradually add milk, stirring with a wire whisk, until soup begins to thicken.
4. Add corn, salt, pepper, nutmeg, soy sauce, and cayenne. Simmer 15 minutes.
5. Before serving, add lemon juice and garnish with parsley or dill. (Add water if soup is too thick.)

Note: Penny adds a 6-ounce can of crab meat with the corn to this soup.

Canadian Cheddar-Cheese Soup ✕✕

Serves 4
Total time: 20 minutes   **Janet**

We're all big Cheddar cheese eaters. This soup stretches a little bit a long way.

2 tbsp. butter
½ onion, chopped
2 tbsp. all-purpose flour
1 cup beef stock (or canned consommé)
2 cups milk
1 cup grated Cheddar cheese
½ tsp. Worcestershire sauce
Juice of ½ lemon
Pinch cayenne
Salt and pepper to taste
½ tsp. mustard
Chopped parsley or chives for garnish

1. In a saucepan, melt butter. Add the onion and sauté until soft. Stir in the flour.
2. Add beef stock and milk. Heat to just below a boil but don't let it boil.
3. Add cheese, Worcestershire sauce, lemon juice, cayenne, salt, pepper, and mustard, stirring constantly until all the cheese has melted. Again, do not let the soup boil.
4. Sprinkle with chopped parsley or chives and serve.

Gnawed Chicken Bone Broth

Serves any number
Total time: 2 hours **Janet**

This recipe couldn't be made in a restaurant because of department of health regulations, but in most families there is a certain amount of togetherness – and besides, the hot water does kill germs.

Leftover chicken bones
Celery leaves
Wilted celery
Chopped onion
Chicken giblets (optional)
Salt and pepper to taste
1 stalk celery, finely chopped
1 lemon, sliced, for garnish
Sprigs of fresh parsley for garnish

1. In a large pot, place all the gnawed bones from the chicken your family ate for dinner. Cover with water and simmer. It's best to leave the bones on the back of the stove to simmer for a day or two, or until you get time to make the soup.
2. Add celery leaves and any wilted celery you have around. Just throw it in; don't bother to chop it.
3. Add just a trace of onion and the giblets of the chicken, if you didn't put them in the gravy.
4. Cook until the bones are white and clean.
5. Strain the soup.
6. Return soup to pot. Add salt, pepper, and finely chopped celery. Cook until the celery is just tender but has not lost its crunchiness.
7. Serve with a slice of lemon and a sprig of fresh parsley in each bowl.

Note: Keep the soup simmering for another meal or store in the fridge.

Leek and Potato Soup

Serves 10 to 15
Total time: 4 hours and 15 minutes   **Janet**

An elegant yet versatile soup, this can be a main luncheon dish in the winter or a cold starter in summer. It's a variation of vichyssoise, the main difference being that in vichyssoise the green part of the leeks is not used so the soup stays snowy white.

4 large potatoes, peeled and sliced
4 large leeks, washed and sliced (including green tops)
2 stalks celery, sliced
10 cups chicken stock (or bouillon cubes with water, if necessary)
Salt and freshly ground pepper to taste
1 tbsp. thyme

1. Place all ingredients in a large oven-proof dish.
2. Cover and cook in a 350 F oven for 3 to 4 hours or until potatoes are softened.
3. Put the whole thing in the blender, in two batches if necessary. Blend until smooth.
4. Serve as is, or sprinkle pieces of toasted French bread with grated cheese. Put them under the broiler for a minute or so and serve on the side.

Note: You can make a less hearty soup by adding milk, cream, yogurt, or a little buttermilk. Serve hot or cold.

Emerald Spinach Soup

Serves 6 to 8
Total time: 30 minutes **Janet**

We invented this soup to use up a cup or so of leftover spinach. Despite its mundane beginnings, it is so pretty it looks as if it were painted.

3 tbsp. butter
1 onion, chopped
2 cups lightly cooked spinach
4 cups chicken broth (or bouillon cubes and water)
1 cup yogurt, milk, or cream
Salt and pepper to taste
Pinch nutmeg

1. In a saucepan, melt the butter. Add onion and sauté until golden (not brown).
2. Place sautéd onions in a blender. Add spinach and blend until smooth.
3. Return mixture to saucepan. Add chicken broth and mix. Add yogurt, milk, or cream. Add salt, pepper, and nutmeg. Serve immediately.

Note: Practically any vegetable can be turned into soup using this method. If you don't plan to use yogurt or milk, thicken by adding a little flour to the melted butter. Yogurt and buttermilk give the soup a lemony tang.

Feather-Light Matzo Balls

Serves 4
Total time: 1 hour and 30 minutes   **Paula**

An excellent lunch dish. Serve in clear, homemade chicken soup with some chopped celery, onion, and fresh parsley.

   4 egg whites
   2 tbsp. butter, melted
   Salt and pepper to taste
   1 cup matzo meal
   2 tbsp. water
   4 egg yolks, beaten
   4 cups boiling, salted water

1. Beat egg whites till frothy and stiff. Set aside.
2. In a bowl, combine melted butter, salt, pepper, matzo meal, 2 tbsp. water, and egg yolks.
3. Gently fold matzo mixture into egg whites and refrigerate for at least 1 hour.
4. When mixture is cold, gently scoop out a portion about the size of a billiard ball. Firmly pat it into a ball (do not overhandle it) and cook in boiling, salted water for 10 minutes.
5. Transfer cooked balls to hot chicken soup and cook for another 10 minutes till light and fluffy.

SALADS

Autumn Picnic

*Chicken Pâté and Melba Toast *by Patsy*

*Peter's Pickled Peppers *by Peter*

*Southern Fried Chicken *by Janet*

*Johnnycake (cornbread) *by Pamela*

***Raw Carrot and Beet Salad** *by Patsy*

*Orange Pumpkin Pie *by Perri*

Raw Carrot and Beet Salad

Serves 6
Total time: 20 minutes **Patsy**

This sensational fibre-filled salad takes only minutes to make if you grate the carrots and beets in a food processor.

Salad:
   3 carrots, grated
   2 raw beets, grated
   ½ cup chopped parsley
   1 cup toasted sunflower seeds

Dressing:
   ¾ cup olive oil
   ½ tsp. dry mustard
   ¼ cup lemon juice
   ½ tsp. cumin powder
   ½ tsp. cumin seed
   Salt and pepper to taste
   Sugar
   Dash Worcestershire sauce
   1 clove garlic, crushed

1. In a bowl, combine carrots and beets. Stir. Add parsley and sunflower seeds. Toss.
2. In a small bowl, combine dressing ingredients. Mix well.
3. Pour dressing over salad. Toss.

Grapefruit and Avocado Salad

Serves 4
Total time: 1 hour and 15 minutes   **Janet**

This light salad is excellent after a hot or substantial main course, such as pepper steak, for it cleanses the palate nicely.

Dressing:
- ½ cup olive oil
- ½ cup sour cream
- 1 tbsp. honey
- Juice of ½ lemon
- Juice of ½ grapefruit
- ½ tsp. salt

Salad:
- 1 head butter lettuce
- 2 ripe avocados, sliced
- 2 fresh grapefruits, sectioned

1. Place all dressing ingredients in the blender and whip until smooth.
2. On a plate, make a bed of lettuce leaves. Alternate slices of avocado and sections of grapefruit in a spiral or a circle on the lettuce. Cover with the dressing.
3. Chill the salad. Add dressing just before serving.

Modified Caesar Salad

Serves 12 to 15
Total time: 2 hours   **Pierre**

This salad is best served before the main course. It's a substantial dish (it makes a good main course for a light lunch), and people cannot do justice to it later in the meal. We don't often serve buffet-style, but if there's a large group we make this salad available before the rest of the meal goes on the sideboard. Otherwise, the guests have to heap their salad on top of the scalloped potatoes and ham. This salad doesn't deserve such treatment.

Dressing:
   1 egg
   1 cup olive oil
   ⅓ cup wine vinegar
   Juice of ½ lemon
   1 cup grated Cheddar cheese
   1 tsp. dry English mustard
   1 tsp. sugar
   1 tsp. salt
   1 tsp. oregano
   2 tbsp. Worcestershire sauce
   4 pinches cayenne pepper
   3 cloves garlic, minced
   1 tsp. fresh ground black pepper

Salad:
   ½ pound lean side bacon
   1 cup cubed bread slices (or croutons)
   Salt and pepper to taste
   3 heads romaine lettuce
   ¼ cup grated Parmesan cheese

1. To make dressing: place the egg in boiling water. Cook for 1 minute only. Peel the egg and place it and all the other dressing ingredients in a blender. Whip until smooth.
2. The original Caesar salad calls for anchovies. I much prefer bacon. Fry until crisp. Drain it on absorbent paper, crumble it into the tiniest possible pieces, then chill it in the freezing compartment of your refrigerator.
3. Put bread cubes into the same pan in which the bacon cooked and sauté them in the bacon fat until they are golden brown and crisp. (If you use croutons bought at the store, you should sauté them in the bacon fat.) Sprinkle croutons with salt and pepper. Drain, then chill in the freezer with the bacon.
4. The only possible lettuce for this salad is romaine: all other kinds wilt too easily, and crispness is essential. Remove the wilted outer leaves. Chop a bit off the top and remove the stalk. Wash lettuce heads and dry carefully, then cut the heads crosswise in one-inch slices. Chill in the refrigerator (not in the freezing compartment).
5. Just before your guests sit down, put the romaine pieces into a chilled salad bowl. Add the bacon and the dressing. Toss. Add croutons. Toss again, then sprinkle with the Parmesan cheese. Serve at once, preferably on chilled glass plates with frosted forks.

Crunchy Spinach Salad

Serves 4 to 6
Total time: 1 hour and 20 minutes   **Pierre**

Pamela always grows spinach in the family garden. When spinach season hits, we stop eating Caesar salad and eat spinach salad. The spinach must be young and tender, and the ingredients must be chilled.

> **2 packages fresh leaf spinach**
> **½ pound lean side bacon**
> **2 eggs, hard-boiled**
> **Caesar Salad Dressing (see pp. 76-77)**

1. Remove spinach stalks. Wash and dry leaves carefully. Tear into small pieces. Chill.
2. Fry and crumble the bacon as for Caesar salad. Chop the eggs. Chill the chopped eggs and the bacon.
3. To serve, place spinach in a chilled salad bowl. Add bacon, egg, and dressing. Toss and serve at once on chilled plates.

Wonderful Watercress Salad

Serves 4
Total time: 15 minutes   **Patsy**

I like watercress because I know it is packed with lots of vitamins, but some people find the salad too nippy or strong. If this is the case, mix it with romaine lettuce.

Salad:
> **1 bunch watercress**
> **½ cup fresh walnuts, chopped**
> **1 green pepper, sliced in strips**

Dressing:
> **2 tbsp. dill**

¼ cup vegetable oil
3 tbsp. cider vinegar
1 tbsp. yogurt
½ tsp. dry mustard
1 clove garlic
Sugar
Salt and pepper to taste

1. Wash watercress and cut stems in half for easier eating. Place in a salad bowl. Add walnuts and pepper.
2. Combine all dressing ingredients in a blender. Mix until thick and smooth. Taste and season.
3. Pour dressing over salad. Toss and serve immediately.

Red Cabbage Salad ✗ ✗

Serves 8
Total time: 1 hour and 15 minutes   **Janet**

This salad is designed to be served with cold meats and pickles at an outdoor summer luncheon buffet.

4 cups finely shredded red cabbage
1 clove garlic, chopped
1 tsp. salt
2 tsp. sugar
2 tbsp. lemon juice
2 tsp. prepared mustard
¼ tsp. paprika
2 tbsp. caraway seeds
1 tbsp. pickled horseradish
1 cup sour cream

1. Place cabbage in a bowl. In another bowl, combine garlic, salt, sugar, lemon juice, mustard, paprika, caraway seeds, and horseradish. Mix well.
2. Pour dressing mixture over cabbage. Toss. Add sour cream. Toss again. Chill.
Note: If you are counting calories, substitute yogurt for the sour cream.

Summer Salad

Peter

This simplified salade niçoise has a subtle flavour.

Salad:
    2 English cucumbers, peeled
    4 stalks celery with leaves, chopped
    4 large tomatoes, cut into bite-sized pieces
    ½ cup finely chopped parsley

Dressing:
    ¼ cup vinegar
    ⅓ cup olive oil
    ½ tsp. garlic salt
    Salt and pepper to taste
    ½ tsp. celery seed
    ½ tsp. dry mustard
    Dash of Worcestershire sauce
    1 tsp. oregano
    1 tsp. basil

Garnish:
    1 cup black olives
    2 hard-boiled eggs

1. Cut cucumber into three-quarter-inch slices; cut slices into quarters.
2. Put cucumber, celery, tomatoes, and parsley into a large salad bowl. Set aside.
3. To make dressing, in a small bowl, combine all dressing ingredients. Blend with a fork until smooth.
4. Pour dressing over salad.
5. With two wooden spoons, crush tomatoes, celery and cucumber. This causes the vegetable juices to mix with the dressing and enhance the flavour. Don't worry about over-crushing.
6. Add black olives and toss.
7. Chill salad in the refrigerator for 30 minutes.
8. Cut eggs into quarters and add before serving.

Cooked Beet Salad

Serves 4 to 6
Total time: 45 minutes **Patsy**

Pretty pink beets are one of my favourite foods, but I detest them when they're pickled; all I can ever taste is vinegar. This is a delicious way to use up leftover cold beets. My secret for leftover vegetable salads is to mix in something green and fresh, like parsley or green pepper. Use your imagination.

Salad:
  4 to 5 large beets, cooked and peeled
  1 green pepper, diced
  ½ cup chopped parsley

Dressing:
  2 tbsp. cider vinegar
  6 tbsp. vegetable oil
  1 tsp. mustard powder
  Pinch sugar
  Salt and pepper to taste
  Rosemary, to taste
  Parsley to taste
  Savory to taste

1. Chop beets into attractive bite-size pieces.
2. Place beets, green pepper, and parsley in a bowl.
3. Place dressing ingredients in the blender. Whip until smooth.
4. Pour dressing over salad. Toss. Chill for 30 minutes before serving.

Party Rice and Bean Salad　✕✕

Serves 12
Total time: 45 minutes and 2 hours to chill　　　**Patsy**

My father likes to serve big slabs of meat and bread. Once I talked him into featuring this salad at a party, and it was eaten up to the last bean. We have to consider the vegetarians!

Salad:
　　3 carrots, chopped
　　6 cups cooked brown rice
　　3 cups cooked kidney beans
　　3 celery stalks, chopped
　　1 green pepper, chopped
　　1 cup cooked, chopped broccoli
　　1 cup chopped parsley
　　½ cup minced scallions (optional)

Dressing:
　　¾ cup olive oil
　　¼ cup lemon juice
　　2 tbsp. minced or crushed garlic
　　Sugar to taste
　　Salt and pepper to taste
　　1 tsp. mustard
　　2 tsp. cumin powder
　　1 tsp. cumin seed
　　2 tsp. curry powder, or more to taste
　　1 tsp. ginger powder, or more to taste

1. Steam carrots for 2 minutes.
2. In a bowl, mix all salad ingredients together.
3. Place dressing ingredients in a small bowl. Mix well.
4. Pour dressing over salad and toss thoroughly. Chill for several hours. You'll smell the garlic every time you open the fridge. It's divine!

Muskoka Rice Salad

Serves 6 to 8
Total time: Overnight   **Penny**

At the cottage, I often put this salad together in the evening or early morning to have on hand at lunchtime when it's hot and sunny and nobody feels like being in the kitchen. It's also great for picnics.

Salad:
   1 cup green beans, cut in half-inch pieces
   ¾ cup diced carrots
   ¾ cup diced red onion
   ⅓ cup diced celery
   ⅓ cup diced green pepper
   4 tbsp. parsley, minced
   4½ cups cooked brown rice

Dressing:
   ⅓ cup Parmesan cheese
   ⅓ cup olive oil
   ¼ cup tarragon vinegar
   2 tbsp. Dijon mustard
   Salt and pepper to taste
   Fresh basil, chopped (optional)

Garnish:
   Tamari soy sauce

1. Steam beans and carrots for about 3 minutes, then rinse in cold water.
2. In a bowl, combine all salad ingredients.
3. In a small bowl, combine dressing ingredients. Whisk well.
4. Pour dressing over salad. Mix well with a wooden spoon. Chill.
5. Serve with Tamari soy sauce.

Lotus Salad

Serves any number
Total time: 1 hour

Penny

This salad makes a colourful and festive presentation for an outdoor buffet. It was inspired by the elaborate offerings that Balinese women make for temple festivals. Created with a combination of flowers and food, the offerings are carried to the temple on the woman's head, blessed by the priest, and then carried back home for dinner!

Equal amounts of:
    Green beans, cut in thirds crosswise
    Broccoli, cut into flowerets
    Cauliflower, cut into flowerets
    Fresh spinach leaves, washed and dried
    Bibb lettuce leaves
    Grated carrots
    Hard-boiled eggs, cut in wedges
    Tomatoes, cut in wedges
    Boiled potatoes, cut in wedges

Garnish:
    Toasted ground sesame seeds
    Alfalfa sprouts
    Creamy Yogurt Dressing (see p. 94)

1. Lightly steam the green beans, broccoli, and cauliflower.
2. On a large round tray or platter, arrange layers of spinach and lettuce in alternating concentric circles, starting from the outside and working toward the centre.
3. Fill centre leaf with grated carrot.
4. Around the centre, make a circle of egg wedges, cut sides facing inward; then a circle of tomatoes, then one of potatoes.
5. Around the potatoes, arrange a circular row of green beans, then cauliflower, then broccoli. Then make another layer of potatoes and so on. Continue to the outside edge of the platter. The amount of vegetables and size of the platter will determine how many circles you end up with.

6. Sprinkle with toasted ground sesame seeds and alfalfa sprouts. Serve with a jug of Creamy Yogurt Dressing, which guests can spoon on themselves.

Note: This can be a meal in itself. You can vary the amounts and kinds of vegetables to suit your needs.

Dilled Carrot Salad

Serves 6
Total time: 1 to 2 hours **Patsy**

When I was a kid, I used to try to feed my carrots to the dog under the table. Even today, I'm not fond of cooked carrots — except in this salad.

Salad:
  6 carrots, washed and cut into small julienne sticks
  1 red pepper, cut into thin strips

Dressing:
  ½ cup olive oil
  2 tbsp. lemon juice
  1 tsp. mustard
  ½ cup dill
  Dash sugar
  Salt and pepper to taste
  1 tbsp. toasted sesame seeds

1. Immerse carrot strips in boiling water for 1 minute. Drain and chill.
2. Place all dressing ingredients in blender. Blend until thick and smooth.
3. Pour dressing over carrots. Mix well. Stir in red pepper. Chill in the refrigerator for 1 to 2 hours before serving.

Low-Cal Green-Bean Salad

Serves 6
Total time: One morning **Paula and Peter**

Peter and I love Edna Staebler's bean salad but on our diet we couldn't have sour cream. This salad has no sour cream or oil, so it's very low in calories.

Salad:
　　1 pound fresh green beans
　　4 slices large Spanish onion
　　1 tsp. finely chopped parsley

Dressing:
　　⅓ cup skim-milk yogurt
　　2 tbsp. white vinegar
　　2 tsp. caraway seeds
　　Salt and pepper to taste
　　½ tsp. garlic salt or grated garlic
　　½ tsp. dry mustard
　　½ tsp. Worcestershire sauce
　　1 onion, finely chopped

1. Clip off tops of beans and string them if necessary. Cook in boiling water for 5 minutes. Drain and rinse with cold water. Refrigerate. (This should be done the morning before serving. If you are in a hurry, soak the cooked beans in ice water.)
2. Sprinkle onion slices with salt. Leave for 5 minutes. Squeeze slices. Add onions and juice and parsley to beans.
3. In a separate bowl, combine all dressing ingredients. Blend with a whisk.
4. Pour dressing over salad. Toss. Refrigerate.

Dandelion Salad

Serves 8
Total time: 15 minutes and 1 hour to chill   **Pamela**

As soon as the ground thaws, the first dandelion leaves are ready to eat. Pick the young leaves before the flowers develop or they become bitter. They taste like endive or escarole. When I serve this, some members of the family complain that I'm feeding them weeds again, but there are rarely any leftovers.

> **8 strips bacon**
> **¼ cup olive oil, if necessary**
> **Freshly ground pepper**
> **1 tsp. dry mustard**
> **¼ cup wine vinegar**
> **1 tsp. honey**
> **2 quarts young dandelion leaves, carefully washed**
> **½ cup diced Spanish onion**
> **Salt to taste**

1. Fry bacon until crisp. Remove from pan, drain, and crumble. Leave the grease in the pan. There should be about ½ cup. If there isn't, add olive oil.
2. To the hot bacon grease, add pepper and mustard and cook for a few seconds. Add vinegar and honey. Stir.
3. In a large salad bowl, mix the dandelion leaves, bacon, and onion.
4. Pour hot dressing over greens. Toss with a fork.
5. Salt to taste. Serve immediately, or chill for an hour or so.

Korean Grocer's Salad

Serves 2
Total time: 15 minutes **Peggy Anne**

Near my home in Manhattan, there are dozens of Korean grocery stores where I do my shopping. They have beautiful displays of Oriental produce.

4 small or 2 large tomatoes
½ ripe Haas avocado
2 carrots
3 Kirby cucumbers
2 pickling onions
3 bamboo shoots from a can
Artichoke hearts in water (optional)
½ fennel root
Basil leaves, coarsely chopped, for garnish
Parsley, coarsely chopped, for garnish
Pepper Vinaigrette (see p. 94)

1. Chop tomatoes, avocado, carrots, cucumbers, onions, bamboo shoots, artichoke hearts, and fennel in bite-sized chunks. Place in a bowl.
2. Pour dressing over vegetables. Top with basil and parsley.

Gazpacho Salad

Serves any number
Total time: 30 minutes and 1 hour to chill   **Pamela**

I make this when vegetables come into their own in August. It travels well to picnics or the cottage.

Salad:
    1 cup diced tomato
    1 cup diced cucumber
    1 cup diced celery
    1 cup diced green pepper
    1 cup diced sweet red onion
    ½ cup chopped fresh basil leaves
    ½ cup chopped fresh dill weed

Dressing:
    ⅓ cup lime juice
    ½ tsp. dry mustard
    ⅓ cup olive oil
    Salt and pepper to taste

1. In a large bowl, mix all salad ingredients.
2. In a jar with a tight lid, shake the lime juice and mustard together. Add olive oil and shake again.
3. Add salt and pepper to taste. If the dressing seems too tart, add a little water and shake again.
4. Pour dressing over salad. Chill at least one hour before serving.

Asparagus Salad

Serves 10
Total time: 15 minutes **Patsy**

Asparagus is one of the most prolific crops in the garden at home. And there is always lots left over after dinner. This is good hot or cold.

2 pounds asparagus
1 to 2 tbsp. butter
½ cup yogurt
1 to 2 cloves garlic, crushed
2 tbsp. lemon juice
Pinch sugar
3 tbsp. fresh dill
1 red pepper, cut in thin julienne strips

1. Wash asparagus, then steam it for about 10 minutes, until tender but still bright green.
2. In a blender, place yogurt and garlic. Blend. Add butter, lemon, sugar, and dill. Blend again.
3. Place hot asparagus on a large flat serving plate. Pour sauce on top. Place red pepper over asparagus decoratively.

Bunny Salad

Serves 2
Total time: 10 minutes   **Penny and Elora**

Here's a quick, nutritious, and fun salad for kids that they can prepare themselves. You'll enjoy it, too.

¼ **cup cooked green beans**
½ **cup grated carrots**
½ **cup alfalfa sprouts**
2 tbsp. raisins
2 tbsp. sunflower seeds, toasted

1. In a small bowl, combine all ingredients.
2. Serve with Creamy Yogurt Dressing (p. 94) or mayonnaise.

Roquefort Salad Dressing

Makes 2 cups
Total time: 15 minutes   **Pierre**

Roquefort dressing goes with any salad but I think it is best on a simple salad. A chilled wedge of head lettuce is ideal.

    1 cup olive oil
    ¼ cup red wine vinegar
    1 cup crumbled Roquefort cheese
    2 tbsp. Worcestershire sauce
    1 tsp. oregano
    4 dashes cayenne pepper
    1 clove garlic, minced
    1 tsp. salt
    ½ tsp. sugar
    1 tsp. freshly ground black pepper
    Juice of ½ lemon

1. Place all ingredients in the blender. Whip until smooth.

Cumin Dressing

Makes 1¹/₂ cups
Total time: 10 minutes   **Penny**

This unusual blend of flavours makes a surprisingly delicate and creamy dressing with a subtle hint of the Orient. I like it with Boston lettuce.

    1 cup olive oil
    ¼ cup tarragon vinegar
    Juice of ½ lemon
    1 clove garlic, chopped

2 tbsp. Dijon mustard
1 tsp. cumin powder
Salt and freshly ground black pepper

1. Place all ingredients in a food processor. Whip until
   smooth.

Tangy Tomato Salad Dressing

Makes 2 cups
Total time: 15 minutes **Eric**

No matter in which order these ingredients are mixed, they
always produce the same pleasing result. A strong-tasting dressing, this is perfect for Romaine lettuce that is a little past its
prime.

10 ounces V-8 or vegetable juice
½ cup olive oil
⅓ cup red wine vinegar
**10 leaves fresh basil, finely chopped, or 1 tbsp. dried
    basil**
2 cloves fresh garlic, minced
1 tsp. dried parsley

1. Place all ingredients in blender. Blend well.

Pepper Vinaigrette

Makes 1 cup
Total time: 10 minutes **John**

This nippy salad dressing goes well with leaf or Boston lettuce.

½ cup vegetable oil
¼ cup cider vinegar
3 cloves garlic
40 peppercorns
1 tsp. Worcestershire sauce
1 tbsp. Dijon mustard
Salt to taste
1 ice cube

1. Place all ingredients in a blender. Whip until smooth.

Creamy Yogurt Dressing

Makes 1¼ cups
Total time: 10 minutes **Penny**

This dressing goes well with Romaine lettuce or cabbage, since it's a little heavier than a vinaigrette.

½ cup safflower oil
2 tbsp. cider vinegar
¼ cup plain yogurt
1 clove garlic
1 tbsp. fresh dill
Salt and freshly ground pepper

1. Combine all ingredients in a blender. Mix until smooth.

FISH

MENU

West Coast Holiday

*Hibachi Oysters *by Peter*

*Crunchy Spinach Salad *by Pierre*

*Poached Salmon in Egg and Caper Sauce

by Janet and Pierre

Corn on the cob *by Perri*

Sliced cucumbers and dill *by Pamela*

Boiled potatoes *by Paul*

*Blackberry Pie *by Penny*

Poached Salmon in Egg and Caper Sauce

Serves 6 to 8
Total time: 1 hour

Janet and Pierre

Since Ian Sclanders, the Maritime writer, used to say that no civilized human being would ever eat poached salmon without egg and caper sauce, we've always served the sauce whether the salmon comes from the Atlantic or the Pacific. I catch coho every summer off Pender Harbour in British Columbia, and each August we are faced with a surfeit of salmon. In winter, however, we buy the Atlantic variety, unfrozen. The salmon is the most festive of all Canadian fish and the Atlantic salmon, unfrozen, the best of all in our opinion. The secret is not to overcook it.

> **1 onion, chopped**
> **1 stalk celery, chopped**
> **½ cup white wine**
> **2 cups water**
> **4 pounds salmon**
> **2 tbsp. butter**
> **½ cup all-purpose flour**
> **2 cups milk**
> **½ cup capers**
> **4 hard-boiled eggs, chopped fine**
> **White pepper and salt to taste**
> **Grated cheese for garnish (optional)**
> **Chopped parsley for garnish (optional)**
> **Lemon slices for garnish**

1. In a poacher, combine onion, celery, white wine, and water. Poach salmon in this fluid until the fish just flakes (10 minutes for each inch of thickness at the thickest part).
2. Meanwhile, make a white sauce. In a saucepan, melt butter. Work in the flour, then stir in the milk at simmering heat. Add some of the poaching liquid to the sauce and stir in capers, hard-boiled egg, pepper, and salt.
3. You can serve the salmon plain with the sauce, or you can brown it under the broiler and dust it with grated cheese and parsley. Garnish it with lemon slices.

Note: Don't use an aluminum pan for the sauce; the mixture of wine and aluminum may turn your sauce grey.

Turbot Charged ✗ ✗

Serves 4
Total time: 45 minutes **Paul**

I eat this often because it is relatively cheap and a cinch to prepare. The delicate taste of the turbot is enhanced by the vegetable juice.

4 turbot fillets
2 tbsp. paprika
2 tbsp. pepper
½ green pepper, cut into bite-sized pieces
2 cooking onions, cut into bite-sized pieces
2 carrots, cut into bite-sized pieces
15 mushrooms, cut in halves
1 stalk broccoli, broken in flowerets
15 green beans, sliced
1 cup white wine
1 cup water

1. Place the turbot in a flat cooking dish. Sprinkle with paprika and pepper.
2. Cover fish with green pepper, onion, carrots, mushrooms, broccoli, and green beans.
3. Pour wine and water over everything. Bake in a 350 F oven for 30 minutes. Baste regularly.

Fast Fish Chowder

Serves 8
Total time: 20 minutes **Pamela**

I live on this in the winter, since I always seem to get home after the supermarkets are closed. Most of the ingredients can be bought at your corner store. It is becoming a Christmas Eve tradition – not too rich to eat in the excitement before the Big Day. It is also easy to expand for a crowd.

> 1 tbsp. vegetable oil
> 2 tbsp. butter
> 2 onions, diced
> 2 celery sticks with leaves, diced
> 2 large unpeeled potatoes, diced
> 2 cloves garlic, minced
> 2 28-ounce cans tomatoes
> 1 pound frozen Boston Bluefish fillets
> 1 green pepper, diced
> 1 tsp. basil (or 2 fresh leaves)
> 1 tsp. dill weed (or 1 tbsp. fresh)
> Salt to taste
> Grated Cheddar or Swiss cheese
> Freshly ground pepper

1. In a large, heavy saucepan, melt the oil and butter. Sauté the onions, celery, potatoes, and garlic.
2. Add the tomatoes and bring to a boil.
3. Add the frozen fish fillets and simmer slowly until fish is thawed.
4. Stir in the green pepper, basil, and dill; flake the fish and add salt to taste.
5. Top with grated Cheddar or Swiss cheese and freshly ground pepper.
6. Serve with slabs of fresh brown bread on the side.

Note: To dress the dish up, add scallops and shrimps, but don't get fancy with a more delicate fish. It will turn to mush.

Clam Chowder Supreme

Serves 6
Total time: 1 hour   **Pierre**

The family wolfs this hearty dish with garlic bread when they come in from skiing or shovelling the walk. Its resuscitative powers are phenomenal.

    2 10-ounce cans butter clams
    1 cup chicken broth
    1 tsp. thyme
    1 tsp. celery salt
    1 tsp. paprika
    1 tsp. freshly ground pepper
    2 large potatoes, diced
    5 slices bacon
    2 medium-sized onions
    ½ cup dry white wine
    3 cups milk
    1 tsp. Madras curry powder
    Pinch cayenne
    Salt to taste
    12 soda crackers

1. In a saucepan, heat the nectar from the clams. Add chicken broth, thyme, celery salt, paprika, and pepper. Stir well.
2. Add the potatoes. Reduce heat to simmer.
3. In a skillet, fry bacon. Add onions, then clams. When onions are soft, add contents of skillet to the saucepan.
4. Add wine and simmer until potatoes are soft.
5. Stir in the milk. Add curry, cayenne, and salt. Serve with crumbled crackers.

Note: This chowder improves with age and can be kept for several days in the fridge.

Sweet-and-Sour Shark Steaks

Serves 4
Total time: 3 hours   **Paul**

This is a natural way to make sweet-and-sour sauce. It is a far cry from the sickly sweet, glue-like substance you find in some Chinese restaurants.

>   1 cup vegetable oil
>   3 cloves garlic, chopped
>   ½ cup red wine
>   4 shark steaks
>   2 tbsp. butter
>   ½ fresh pineapple, cut in pieces
>   2 firm tomatoes, cut in pieces
>   3 cooking onions, cut in pieces
>   ½ green pepper, cut in pieces
>   ⅔ cup soy sauce
>   ½ cup pineapple juice
>   Juice from 1 lemon

1. In a bowl, combine oil, garlic, and wine. Add shark and marinate for 2 hours.
2. In a large wok, melt butter over low heat. Add pineapple, tomatoes, onions, and pepper. Cook until tender.
3. Add soy sauce and pineapple juice. Simmer for 5 minutes.
4. Remove shark steaks from marinade. Cook on a barbeque until crisp and firm.
5. Serve shark with sauce. Top with lemon juice.

Flashfire Shrimp   ✕ ✕

Serves 4
Total time: 1 hour   **Paul**

Hellishly hot, but heavenly good.

4 dozen large shrimp
1 large bowl ice water
1 tsp. salt
3 tbsp. butter
5 cloves garlic, minced
⅓ cup ginger, minced
5 small dried red chili peppers and seeds, minced
⅓ cup cooking oil
15 green onions, cut into 2-inch pieces
⅓ cup grated lemon rind
⅔ cup lemon juice
⅔ cup soy sauce

1. Peel the shrimps (I never devein them) and place them in the ice water with salt. Soak for 30 minutes.
2. In a large wok, melt butter. Sauté garlic, ginger, and chilies lightly. Remove the mixture from the wok.
3. Drain shrimp.
4. In wok, heat oil over high heat. When the oil is hot but not smoking (be careful), add the drained shrimp all at once. Stir vigorously for 30 seconds.
5. Add garlic mixture, green onions, and lemon rind. Stir for another 30 seconds. Add lemon juice and soy sauce.
6. Serve immediately with a bowl of steamed white rice.
Note: The shrimp will continue to cook at the table.

Spicy Coconut Fish

Serves 4
Total time: 35 minutes   **Patsy**

In Indonesia, they use coconut cream for everything, but they throw out the coconut water. The women make the cream by boiling the coconut meat and squeezing it, then straining it through a sieve. Here, you can buy the cream in a can.

¼ cup vegetable oil
2 onions, chopped
3 cloves garlic, crushed
2 tbsp. grated ginger
2 tsp. coriander powder
1 to 2 tsp. minced fresh green or red chili (or to taste)
2 cups coconut cream
2 pounds fish fillets
Diced green pepper (optional)
2 tbsp. lemon juice
1 tsp. brown sugar

1. In a heavy skillet or wok, heat oil. Sauté onions, garlic, ginger, coriander, and chili over medium heat, stirring constantly.
2. Add coconut cream. Cook till heated. Add fillets and green pepper and simmer on low heat for 5 to 10 minutes, or until fish is no longer transparent.
3. Add lemon juice and brown sugar. Serve on a bed of rice.

Note: To make coconut cream, take ½ pound of unsweetened dessicated coconut and boil in 2 cups of water for 5 to 10 minutes. Turn heat down and simmer for about 15 minutes; then let it cool. Squeeze the water out of the coconut with your hand, or use a fine sieve. It can also be thinned down with water.

Barbecued Salmon Marinade

Serves 6
Total time: 1 hour and 20 minutes   **Rico**

The interesting thing about this recipe is that the lemon actually cooks the fish if it is marinated for a while. The fish can therefore be put on the fire just long enough to braise it nicely on both sides, thus avoiding the cardinal sin among salmon eaters: dry, overcooked salmon!

½ **cup water**
½ **cup lemon juice**
2 **tbsp. Tamari soy sauce**
2 **tbsp. crushed garlic**
¼ **cup vegetable oil**
6 **salmon steaks or fillets**

1. In a large bowl or flat dish, combine water, lemon juice, soy sauce, garlic, and oil.
2. Add fish and marinate for 1 hour. (It's best to submerge the fish. If the fish is not covered, turn it 3 or 4 times.)
3. Remove fish from marinade and barbecue over a medium fire until just browned.

Shrimps and Snow Peas in Coconut Cream ✘✘✘

Serves 4
Total time: 45 minutes **Penny**

This is my own variation of a typical Indonesian curry dish. As a cheaper alternative to shrimps and snow peas, try using green beans and beansprouts.

1 large onion, chopped
3 cloves garlic, minced
2 tbsp. peeled, grated ginger
1 tbsp. cumin seed
1 tbsp. turmeric (ground or freshly chopped)
1 tbsp. coriander seeds
1 tsp. chopped kencur*
1 tsp. cayenne or 2 small minced green chilies (to
    taste)
1 tsp. trassi* (fish paste)
2 tbsp. vegetable oil
1 cup coconut cream (canned or fresh)
1 stick sere* (lemon grass)
1 pound fresh shrimp, shelled and dried
Oil for frying
1 cup snow peas
4 hard-boiled eggs, halved
Lemon juice to taste

1. With a mortar and pestle or in a food processor, pound or grind onion, garlic, ginger, cumin, turmeric, coriander, kencur, cayenne or chilies, and trassi to a paste.
2. In a skillet or wok, heat oil. Add paste. Sauté for 5 to 10 minutes.
3. Stir in coconut cream and add lemon grass. Simmer briefly.
4. In another frying pan, in a little oil, fry shrimp quickly (2 to 3 minutes). Do not overcook.

5. Add shrimps, snow peas, and hard-boiled eggs to coconut sauce and heat quickly. Add lemon juice. Serve immediately with rice.
   *These ingredients are optional, since they're not always available in North America. They make the recipe more authentic, but it's still delicious without them.

Wounded Pickerel

Serves 8
Total time: 1 hour   **Paul**

If you order steamed fish in Chinatown, this is the way you are likely to get it, except that this recipe has more ginger and garlic and leaves out the monosodium glutamate.

1 large pickerel
1 large ginger root, grated
1 garlic bulb, crushed
25 green onions, slivered
1 lemon
¼ cup vegetable oil
¼ cup soy sauce
½ cup black bean sauce (optional)

1. Scale and gut the pickerel. Cut 4 or 5 diagonal gashes along each side.
2. Put fish in a steamer. Add half the ginger, garlic, and green onions and a few slices of lemon. Steam 20 to 30 minutes.
3. Add remaining ginger, garlic, and green onions. Steam another five minutes.
4. In a saucepan, heat oil till warm. Add soy sauce, juice of remaining lemon, and black bean sauce. Heat and pour over fish before serving.

Cannelloni Stuffed with Crab and Spinach

Serves 4
Total time: 1 hour   **Perri**

This is difficult to make but guests always think I'm a gourmet cook when I serve it.

> 15 lasagna noodles
> 1 bunch spinach
> 1 7-ounce can crab meat, drained
> ½ tsp. olive oil
> ½ tsp. butter
> 1 small onion, finely chopped
> 1 clove garlic, finely chopped
> 1 egg
> 1½ cups Hollandaise sauce (recipe follows)
> 1 tbsp. breadcrumbs
> Salt and pepper to taste
> 1 tsp. grated nutmeg
> 1 cup whipping cream
> 1 cup coarsely grated Parmesan cheese

1. Cook lasagna in boiling water for 5 to 10 minutes, until al dente. Drain.
2. Wash spinach. Place in saucepan. Cover and cook until just tender. Drain off all excess water and chop spinach finely.
3. In a large bowl, combine crab meat and spinach.
4. In a frying pan, heat oil and butter. Sauté onion and garlic until transparent. Add to crab and spinach mixture.
5. To crab and spinach mixture, add egg, ¾ cup Hollandaise sauce, breadcrumbs, salt, pepper, and nutmeg.
6. Cut cooked lasagna noodles into 4-inch pieces. Put a portion of crab and spinach stuffing on each piece and roll into cylinders.
7. Put cylinders in bottom of a casserole dish side by side.
8. Cover with whipping cream, remaining Hollandaise sauce, and Parmesan cheese. Bake in a 350 F oven for 30 minutes.

Hollandaise Sauce

Makes 1¹/₂ cups
Total time: 10 minutes

3 egg yolks
2 tbsp. lemon juice
¹/₂ tsp. salt
¹/₂ tsp. white pepper
¹/₂ cup softened butter
¹/₂ cup boiling water

1. In a blender, place egg yolks, lemon juice, salt, pepper, and butter. Blend well.
2. Remove cover and gradually add boiling water while blender is running. Replace cover and blend for 1 minute, or until sauce is smooth.

Hot Sweet Halibut

Serves 4
Total time: 1 hour **Paul**

This recipe had its beginnings – canned sardines and bread-and-butter pickles – on a day when the cupboard was bare and a snowstorm raged outside.

2 tbsp. oil
2 tbsp. butter
3 onions, diced
3 celery stalks, diced
½ red pepper, diced
½ green pepper, diced
1 carrot, diced
½ pineapple, diced
4 halibut fillets, cut in bite-sized pieces
3 dried red chili peppers
¼ cup lemon juice
3 tbsp. soy sauce

1. In a large wok, heat oil and butter. Sauté onions, celery, peppers, and carrot until soft.
2. Add fish, pineapple, and chilies. Stir-fry until fish is tender.
3. Add lemon juice and soy. Heat and serve.

Pacific Casserole

Serves 8
Total time: 40 minutes   **Pierre**

The family invented this while vacationing on Gabriola Island
in the Gulf of Georgia in July 1962. We caught the salmon and
raked the oysters off the beach.

4 dozen oysters, shelled
1 salmon, 3 to 4 pounds
2 hard-boiled eggs, chopped
½ cup mushrooms, chopped
½ cup oyster liquid
½ cup milk
1 cup cracker crumbs
1 cup grated cheese

1. Lay half the oysters in a large oven-proof casserole.
2. Fillet the salmon and lay it on the oysters.
3. In a bowl, combine eggs and mushrooms. Mix. Add oyster
   liquid and milk to form a sauce.
4. Pour the sauce over the salmon. Cover with the rest of the
   oysters.
5. Add the cracker crumbs and grated cheese.
6. Bake in a 350 F oven for 30 minutes, or until crust is
   brown.

Curried Haddock

Serves 4
Total time: 1 hour **Paul**

Curry rescues this fish, which I usually find too bland and difficult to stir-fry because it turns to mush.

8 tbsp. butter
3 large cooking onions, cut into strips
1 green pepper, cut into strips
1 red pepper, cut into strips
15 medium-sized mushrooms, sliced
6 tbsp. all-purpose flour
1 cup milk
3 tbsp. curry
4 haddock fillets
1 cup wine

1. In a large saucepan, melt 6 tbsp. of the butter. Sauté onions, peppers, and mushrooms until hot but still crisp.
2. Add the flour, stirring constantly over medium heat.
3. Add the milk gradually, stirring constantly until the mixture is thick. Add curry and simmer.
4. Put the fish fillets in an electric frying pan with the remaining 2 tbsp. butter. Cover with wine and poach.
5. Pour the curry-and-vegetable sauce over fish. Simmer for 20 minutes. Serve with rice.

Poor Man's Salmon

Serves 3
Total time: 1 hour

Paul

My father likes steamed salmon with a delicious egg and caper sauce. This is the cheap and easy version, and one of my favourites.

    ¼ cup butter
    3 celery stalks, diced
    3 onions, diced
    ½ green pepper, diced
    ¼ cup all-purpose flour
    1 cup milk
    1 6-ounce can salmon
    ¼ cup capers
    4 hard-boiled eggs, chopped
    1 cup wine
    Juice of 1 lemon
    Grated rind of 1 lemon

1. In a saucepan, heat butter. Sauté celery, onion, and peppers lightly.
2. Add the flour. Stir, then gradually add the milk. Simmer, stirring constantly, until sauce thickens.
3. Add salmon, capers, hard-boiled eggs, and wine. Cook until thickened.
4. Add lemon juice and grated rind.
5. Serve on rice in soup bowls.

Seafood Casserole

Serves 6
Total time: 45 minutes   **Janet**

Grace and the late Jack Scott served us this casserole at their home on Saltspring Island, where we gathered fresh clams off the beach.

1 cup dry white wine
1 onion, sliced
1 tbsp. snipped parsley
2 tbsp. lemon juice
Salt and pepper to taste
1 pound scallops
5 tbsp. butter
6 tbsp. all-purpose flour
1 cup table cream
2 to 3 tbsp. chopped Gruyère cheese
½ pound crab meat
½ pound medium shrimps (uncooked, if possible), peeled
½ pound sliced mushrooms
1½ cups whole-wheat breadcrumbs

1. In a saucepan, combine wine, onion, parsley, lemon juice, salt, and pepper. Bring to a boil. Add scallops and simmer for a minute or so.
2. In another saucepan, melt 4 tbsp. of the butter. Stir in flour.
3. Add scallops with their cooking liquid all at once. Cook, stirring constantly, over medium heat for a minute or so, or until thickened. Add cream, but do not let it boil. Remove from heat.
4. Stir in cheese, crab meat, shrimps, and mushrooms.
5. Transfer to casserole or individual dishes. Combine breadcrumbs with remaining 1 tbsp. butter and put on top of casserole. Bake in a 325 F oven for 15 minutes, or until top browns slightly.

Chicken and Oyster Pie

Serves 6
Total time: 2 hours

Janet

A festive dish for a winter dinner party, this pie may be served without the pastry and over rice if desired.

2 chickens, cut in pieces
6 cups water
2 stalks celery, cut in pieces
1 carrot, cut in pieces
1 onion, cut in quarters
6 peppercorns
½ cup dry white wine
½ cup butter
4 shallots, sliced
½ cup flour
3 egg yolks, beaten
1½ dozen oysters, fresh, frozen, or canned
2 tsp. thyme
2 sprigs fresh parsley
Salt and pepper to taste
Pastry to top (see p. 186)

1. In a large pot, put chicken pieces and water. Add celery, carrot, and onion. Simmer gently for 30 minutes. Let cool.
2. When cool, remove chicken pieces from broth. Take meat from bones and skin from the meat. Set meat aside.
3. In a blender, place 2 cups of the broth and the chicken skin. Blend. Return mixture to broth. Add bones, peppercorns, and wine.
4. Boil until mixture is reduced to about 4 cups. Strain.
5. In a saucepan, melt the butter. Sauté shallots. Blend in flour. Add strained broth. Cook over medium heat, whisking until smooth, for about 2 to 3 minutes.
6. Add a little of the hot sauce to the beaten egg yolks. Stir, then return to the rest of the mixture, whisking constantly.
7. Add chicken meat to sauce, along with the oysters, thyme, parsley, salt and pepper. Put in a deep casserole. Cover with pastry. Bake in a 375 F oven for 20 minutes or until pastry is golden brown.

POULTRY

MENU

Christmas Feast

*The Morton Thompson Turkey and Stuffing
by Pierre

Super Bread Sauce *by Pierre*

Cranberry sauce *by Pamela*

Mashed turnips *by Eric*

Minted peas *by Patsy*

Mashed potatoes and gravy *by Janet*

*Raspberry Meringues *by Pierre*

The Morton Thompson Turkey ✕✕✕

Serves 20 to 25
Total time: Overnight

Pierre

Every Christmas since 1947 in our home we have followed the ritual of making this incredible turkey. The method has been adapted from an original recipe – half French and half Chinese – by the American novelist Morton Thompson. Since we started making it, the recipe has been publicized in the press and on television, and we are bombarded each Yuletide by thousands of requests for copies. Indeed, every Christmas Eve and Christmas Day we find ourselves on the phone discussing the recipe with others who are working on stuffing, paste, and giblet gravy. Some people read the recipe and think it's a joke. Thompson once wrote that it took him five years to convince the readers of his newspaper column the whole thing wasn't a spoof. It isn't. We recommend that if you try the recipe, you leave nothing out: the balance of spices is a delicate one. And do not neglect to baste your bird; that is half the battle.

1 turkey (up to 25 pounds), with neck, heart, gizzard, and liver

Dressing, Bowl #1:
1 apple, peeled, cored, and sliced
1 orange, peeled and sectioned
½ lemon, peeled and sectioned
1 26-ounce can water chestnuts
3 tbsp. preserved ginger
1 26-ounce can crushed pineapple

Dressing, Bowl #2:
4 cloves
2 tsp. dry English mustard
2 tsp. caraway seeds
3 tsp. celery seeds
2 tsp. poppy seeds
2½ tsp. oregano
1 bay leaf, crushed
1 tsp. black pepper
½ tsp. mace

4 tbsp. fresh parsley, chopped
5 cloves garlic, chopped
½ tsp. turmeric
4 large onions, chopped
6 stalks celery, chopped
½ tsp. marjoram
½ tsp. savory
1 tbsp. poultry seasoning
Salt to taste

Dressing, Bowl #3:
Fat from turkey
3 11-ounce packages breadcrumbs
¾ pound ground veal
¼ pound ground pork
½ cup butter

Basting fluid and gravy:
1 bay leaf
1 tsp. paprika
½ tsp. ground coriander
1 clove garlic, chopped
4 cups water
Salt and pepper to taste
1 cup apple cider

Paste cover:
8 egg yolks
2 tbsp. dry English mustard
¼ cup onion juice
2 tsp. salt
½ tsp. cayenne pepper
2 tbsp. lemon juice
Sifted flour

1. Mix all Bowl #1 ingredients thoroughly.
2. Mince cloves after discarding the heads. Mix all Bowl #2 ingredients thoroughly.
3. In a small skillet, render as much fat as possible from the turkey. Mix fat in a bowl with other ingredients from Bowl #3.

4. Mix together all the dressing bowls. "Mix it until your forearms and wrists ache," Thompson wrote. "Then mix it some more. Now toss it enough so it isn't a doughy mass."

5. Chop up the turkey's neck, heart, gizzard, and liver. Place in a saucepan with bay leaf, paprika, coriander, garlic, and water. (Do not add the cider at this point.) Simmer. The longer you simmer this basting fluid, the better. Keep adding water.

6. We make our dressing the night before and simmer our basting fluid all night. If you do that, however, keep the stuffing cool overnight.

7. Rub the bird inside and out with salt and pepper and stuff it reasonably full at both ends. Sew it up, or skewer it and tie the ends. Tie the legs and wings tightly to the body with good strong cord.

8. Place bird on a rack, or place breast-side down on a drip pan. Put in 450 F oven.

9. Mix together the ingredients for the paste cover. Sift in enough flour to make a stiff paste. As soon as the turkey is browned all over from the red-hot oven, haul it out, sizzling. Using a pastry brush, cover it completely with paste. Slip it back into the oven so that the paste will set. Then haul it out again and, in Thompson's words, "paint every nook and cranny of it once more."

10. Turn the oven down to 325 F, put some water in the drip pan, and roast the turkey. The paste will keep the heat in. Never cook the turkey more than nine or ten minutes to the pound.

11. Add the cider to the giblet gravy simmering on the stove. Keep it warm. This is your basting fluid. You should baste the turkey thoroughly every 15 minutes. We use an aluminum baster with a rubber bulb, and we set the timer on the stove alarm to remind us when to baste. And don't forget to keep adding water to the gravy in the pan to keep it from burning.

12. When you remove the turkey from the oven it will be dead black. Don't let that worry you. You can remove the paste, if you want, with tweezers, but we don't bother because beneath that shell the bird will be, in Thompson's words, "succulent, giddy-making with wild aroma, crisp and crunchable and crackling."

13. The gravy in the pan can be thickened with a little flour and cooked on top of the stove. We serve the turkey with Super Bread Sauce (recipe follows) as well as cranberry sauce and usually with Raspberry Meringues (see p. 181) because we have 8 egg whites left over from the paste. As Thompson wrote: "You do not have to be a carver to eat this turkey; speak harshly to it and it will fall apart."

Super Bread Sauce

Serves 10
Total time: 30 minutes **Pierre**

Although not everybody likes bread sauce, I love it and so does the family. We always have it with Christmas turkey, but it's good with any rich game.

1 onion
12 cloves
2 cups milk
2 tbsp. butter
1 cup white breadcrumbs
4 tbsp. table cream
1 tsp. mace
½ tsp. cayenne pepper

1. Peel the onion and stud it with cloves.
2. In a saucepan, place the studded onion, milk, and butter. Bring to a boil.
3. Add breadcrumbs and simmer for 20 minutes.
4. Remove onion. To the sauce, add cream, mace, and cayenne. Beat until smooth. Serve warm.
Note: I sometimes use more mace and often add a little onion juice. It's all a matter of taste and tasting. Mace, incidentally, is the essential ingredient.

Hibachi Chicken ✗✗

Serves 4 to 6
Total time: 1 hour and 30 minutes   **Rico**

This is a simple but effective way to barbecue chicken for those who don't like gooey-sweet barbecue sauces.

1 cup lemon juice
4 cloves garlic, crushed
6 pieces chicken

1. In a bowl, combine lemon juice and garlic. Add chicken pieces and let sit for approximately 1 hour. (Ideally, the chicken should be submerged in the marinade.)
2. Barbecue the chicken over a low fire. The chicken should cook at a leisurely pace. While it cooks, baste the chicken with the marinade.

Honey-Garlic Barbecued Chicken ✗✗

Serves 4
Total time: 3 hours   **Paul**

This is a bit sticky and difficult to handle because of the honey, but the result is well worth the trouble. The honey must be heated first so it will mix easily with other ingredients.

1 cup honey, warmed
1 cup vegetable oil
1 cup white wine
10 cloves garlic, crushed
½ cup crushed ginger
½ cup lemon juice
½ cup soy sauce
½ cup water
⅓ cup pepper
⅓ cup sage
8 chicken breasts

1. Place all ingredients except chicken in a bowl. Mix well.
2. Add chicken and marinate for at least two hours.
3. Place breasts bone-side-down on barbecue over medium-hot coals. When firm, turn skin-side-down to brown.

Deep-Fried Chicken Wings   ✗✗✗

Serves 6
Total time: 1 hour   **Janet**

This is an old favourite. When the children were young, we would sit around the television on a Saturday night watching "Perry Mason" and eat with our fingers. It takes a while to cook enough of these wings for a crowd, so practise on a small group. Allow about five wings for each person.

30 chicken wings
2 cups flour
Salt and pepper
Vegetable oil

1. Separate the wings into three sections; remove the tips and save them for soup. Dredge the two remaining sections in flour seasoned with salt and pepper.
2. In a large, heavy pot or deep fryer, heat 3 inches of cooking oil.
3. Put the wings into the oil in batches of about six. Cook at high heat until wings float. Remove and drain on paper towels.

Ginger Chicken

Serves 4
Total time: Overnight **Penny**

Inspired by Chinese and Balinese cooking, this dish is great for entertaining because it must be made a day ahead. It's delicious served with rice and plain steamed vegetables.

 1 cup dried shiitake mushrooms
 5 scallions
 1¼ cups grated ginger
 4 tbsp. vegetable oil
 4 boneless chicken breasts, skinned, cut into small
      pieces
 1 onion, sliced
 3 cloves garlic, chopped
 2 tbsp. Tamari soy sauce
 1 tbsp. honey

1. Soak mushrooms in warm water for 15 minutes. Then drain and slice them.
2. Cut scallions into half-inch pieces. Soak pieces in a bowl of cold water for 5 minutes.
3. Soak ginger in cold water for 5 minutes. Drain and squeeze out all water; rinse and drain well.
4. In a frying pan or heavy wok, heat oil, then fry chicken pieces quickly. Remove from pan.
5. To the pan, add onion, garlic, and mushrooms; fry for 1 minute. Add ginger. Stir-fry for 2 to 3 minutes.
6. Return chicken to pan. Combine soy sauce and honey and stir into chicken. Drain scallions. Add to pan.
7. Place mixture in a bowl. Cover and refrigerate overnight.
8. To serve, stir-fry quickly to reheat.

Fast Elegant Chicken Breasts

Serves 4
Total time: 15 minutes   **Peter**

Mom once left a note for me on the fridge: "Boneless chicken breasts in fridge. Please feed your father." It seemed a shame just to bake them, so I concocted this dish. I got an indirect compliment a week later when I got a call from Mom, asking for the recipe.

> **2 skinless, boneless chicken breasts, halved**
> **¼ cup all-purpose flour**
> **1 tsp. basil**
> **1 tsp. tarragon**
> **1 tsp. salt**
> **Cracked pepper to taste**
> **2 tbsp. butter**
> **½ cup white wine**
> **Chopped parsley, for garnish**

1. Place chicken breasts between two pieces of waxed paper or plastic wrap. Pound with a mallet until flattened.
2. In a bowl, mix flour, basil, tarragon, salt and pepper.
3. Dust chicken thoroughly with flour mixture.
4. In a skillet, melt butter. Add chicken and cook over high heat for approximately 1 minute on each side.
5. Lower heat to medium. Add wine. Cover and cook for 1 minute.
6. Reduce heat to low. Uncover and cook for about 5 minutes.
7. Serve on a bed of rice with sauce. Sprinkle with chopped parsley.

Note: The aroma created by the tarragon and wine is fantastic.

Chicken Kiev

Serves 4
Total time: 1 hour   **Janet**

Since this dish must be eaten at once, it is rarely possible to make it for more than six people. This may be why it is difficult to get in most restaurants and not easy to find in cookbooks (most of which, for reasons that baffle us, omit the key ingredient: garlic). In Italian restaurants you can sometimes discover it listed as "Chicken Sorpriso." And, if you make it properly, you should indeed be pleasantly surprised by the butter spurting from the hot chicken when you plunge your knife into it.

1½ **cups butter**
3 **cloves garlic, minced**
1 **tbsp. parsley, chopped**
¼ **cup chives, chopped**
1 **tsp. salt**
1 **tsp. fresh ground pepper**
½ **tsp. rosemary**
4 **whole skinless, boneless chicken breasts, halved**
Flour for dredging
3 **eggs, lightly beaten**
1½ **cups breadcrumbs**
Vegetable oil for frying

1. Soften the butter and add the garlic, parsley, chives, salt, pepper, and rosemary. Shape the seasoned butter into four finger-sized rolls and place in freezer until solid.
2. Place chicken breasts between layers of waxed paper or plastic wrap and pound them with a wooden mallet until they are about one-quarter-inch thick. Then place them on a chopping board and cut them into four-inch squares.
3. Dip each square of chicken in flour. Place one roll of frozen butter on top of one chicken square, brush a little beaten egg around the outside edge, and place another square of chicken over the butter. Pinch the edges of the two chicken squares together, then dip into the beaten egg and then into the breadcrumbs. Refrigerate to make the crumbs adhere.

4. Repeat with the remainder of the chicken pieces.
5. Fill a deep fryer or pot with about four inches of vegetable oil and heat to 475 F. Gently place one or two of the chicken squares in the fryer. Cook for about five minutes. The chicken is done when it floats. Lift out gently – with tongs, not with a fork – and serve immediately.

Note: Preparing and frying the chicken is a messy and fiddly job, but it's worth it.

Chicken-Liver Curry

Serves 2
Total time: 30 minutes **Patsy**

Fantastic if you have just a short time to prepare dinner.

3 tbsp. oil
2 tsp. ground ginger
2 tsp. curry powder
1 to 2 tsp. dry mustard
3 cloves garlic, crushed
1 tbsp. grated ginger
1 onion, minced
1 pound chicken livers, washed and cut in half
½ cup green or red pepper
3 tbsp. lemon juice

1. In a heavy skillet or wok, heat oil. Add ground ginger, curry powder, and mustard. Mix well, then add garlic, grated ginger, and onion. Sauté over medium heat until onion is transparent.
2. Add chicken livers. Fry until livers are browned but still pink inside.
3. Add peppers and simmer until peppers are just tender.
4. Add lemon juice and serve with generous portions of brown rice.

Note: A tomato or two can be added with peppers for variety.

Chicken with Rice: Three Variations

✕

Serves 4
Total time: 45 minutes

Paul

When we were kids, Mom used to serve a dish she called Chicken with Rice. It was one of those meals in the casserole category from which my father was always conspicuously absent. When I became older, I referred to this meal as Depression Chicken with Rice, because the poultry in question had already done time in a roasting pan (an earlier meal for Dad), sandwiches (for lunch) and soup (for all of us). By the time the haggard little chicken made a rendezvous with the rice, its gourmet status had considerably diminished. These three dishes are a variation on the original, but still retain the gourmet label, and you can only make sandwiches and soup after the fact.

Chicken Curry

A Ingredients
  2 cups chicken broth
  1 cup white wine
  2 cups water

B Ingredients
  2 celery stalks
  1 green pepper
  1 red pepper
  2 carrots
  3 cooking onions
  1 broccoli stalk
  7 pineapple rings

C Ingredients
  5 tbsp. curry powder
  2 tbsp. tarragon
  2 tbsp. sage
  2 tbsp. rosemary
  2 cups rice
  4 chicken breasts

Chicken Citrus

A Ingredients
  2 cups orange juice
  1 cup lemon juice
  2 cups water

B Ingredients
  2 celery stalks
  1 green pepper
  1 red pepper
  2 carrots
  3 cooking onions
  1 broccoli stalk
  2 oranges (peel optional)
  2 lemons (peel optional)

C Ingredients
  2 tbsp. tarragon
  2 tbsp. sage
  2 tbsp. rosemary
  2 cups rice
  4 chicken breasts

Chicken Italian

A Ingredients
    2 cups tomato juice
    2 cups water

B Ingredients
    2 Italian sausages
    2 celery stalks
    1 green pepper
    1 red pepper
    3 carrots
    3 cooking onions
    1 broccoli stalk
    2 sliced tomatoes

C Ingredients
    2 tbsp. tarragon
    2 tbsp. sage
    2 tbsp. rosemary
    2 cups rice

    4 chicken breasts

1. In a saucepan boil all the A Ingredients.
2. Meanwhile, chop all the B Ingredients into bite-sized chunks.
3. When the liquid is boiling vigorously, throw in all chopped B ingredients, then the C Ingredients, with the rice last. Stir it around, bring to the boil again and reduce to simmer.
4. Place chicken in a casserole or saucepan. Pour liquid, vegetables and rice on top. Put a tight-fitting lid on the pot and let it cook for 30 minutes on top of the stove or in a 350 F oven.

Southern Fried Chicken

Serves 4 to 6
Total time: 30 minutes   **Janet**

An old-fashioned chicken dish – crisp on the outside, moist on the inside.

> **2 chickens**
> **1 cup milk**
> **2 cups all-purpose flour**
> **1 tsp. salt**
> **1 tsp. baking powder**
> **2 tsp. thyme**
> **Cooking oil**

1. Cut up chickens, separating legs and thighs and cutting breasts into two pieces. Remove necks, backs, and wings (these can be saved for soup).
2. Dip chicken pieces in milk, then in flour mixed with salt, baking powder, and thyme.
3. In a heavy pot, pour cooking oil to a depth of about 3 inches. Heat oil but do not allow it to smoke.
4. Dip each piece of chicken again in the flour mixture.
5. Fry chicken in oil (don't overcrowd the pieces), turning once, until they float. Do not overcook. When the juices of the thigh run clear (not bloody) when meat is pricked with a fork, the chicken is done.

MEAT

MENU

Summer Cottage Pig-Out

*Muskoka Sunrise *by Peter*

*Chilled Cucumber Soup *by Pamela*

***Deep-Six Pig** by Pierre*

***Fridge Chutney** by Pamela*

*Muskoka Rice Salad *by Penny*

*Ruby-Red Raspberry Mousse *by Janet*

Deep-Six Pig

Serves 8
Total time: Overnight

Pierre

Arthur Hailey, the novelist, and I cooked a pig like this at his cottage in the Haliburton Highlands in Ontario. It's great for a family holiday.

> 3 cups rice
> 3 tbsp. butter
> 6 large onions, chopped
> 2 cups soy sauce
> 2 bunches fresh celery, chopped
> 6 large apples, peeled, cored, and chopped
> ¼ cup fresh ginger, grated
> 1 suckling pig
> 4 tbsp. dry English mustard
> 1 cup honey

1. Cook the rice until medium soft.
2. In a small skillet, melt butter. Sauté the onions until transparent.
3. In a large bowl, combine onions, rice, 1 cup of the soy sauce, celery, apples, and half the ginger.
4. Stuff pig with onion and rice mixture; sew up the pig.
5. Blend mustard, honey, remaining 1 cup soy sauce and remaining ginger. Using a pastry brush, paint the outside of the pig with mustard-honey sauce.
6. Wrap the pig in tin foil, cover with damp burlap and tie.
7. Slip the wrapped pig through two coat hangers and slide a long pole through the hooks.
8. Bury the pig in a trench lined with rocks and heated red-hot overnight with firewood or charcoal.
9. If the pig goes into the trench at breakfast time, it should be ready to eat by dinnertime. (But have the barbecue

ready just in case.) Use the pole to lift the pig out of the steaming-hot earth.

Note: We always make a ceremony of digging up the pig and bearing it triumphantly to the picnic table. When I cooked such a pig for our local Boy Scout troop, we had a bagpiper to pipe the pig to the table.

Pierre's Pepper Steak

Serves 4
Total time: 30 minutes **Pierre**

We serve this when we have one couple over. It is fun to make and fun to eat — and it can be made at the table.

> **4 tbsp. butter**
> **4 onions, finely chopped**
> **Cracked black pepper**
> **4 6- to 8-ounce steak filets, cut 1¼ inches thick**
> **1 cup red wine**
> **¼ cup brandy**

1. In a skillet, melt butter. Sauté onions until soft. Set aside.
2. Press black pepper into both sides and the edge of the meat.
3. In a clean hot skillet, sear steaks on both sides and cook until half done.
4. Cover with onions and add red wine. Complete cooking steaks to personal taste. (I insist on rare.)
5. In a small skillet, warm the brandy and flame. Pour over steaks and serve.

Note: This piquant dish can be served with a chilled salad and any light fruit dessert.

Fridge Chutney

Makes a variable amount
Total time: 4 hours   **Pamela**

Mom has a fridge like Fibber McGee's closet. It is bad enough
in the winter, but toward the end of the summer it is impossible.
With everything fresh in the garden, yesterday's vegetables are
abandoned to squashed ignominy in the crisper. Half-eaten
eggplant, over-ripe tomato, floppy celery, and dehydrated lemon
wedges fight for space with enormous and ever-present zucchini
and peppers. Mom won't let anybody throw any of it out, since
it is "still perfectly good," so it sits there, growing mould, while
everyone cheerfully picks new stuff from the garden. This fridge-
cleaning recipe has no measurements to speak of and requires
a lot of tasting.

> **Celery, carrots, green and red tomatoes, green and
> red peppers, carrots, lemons, zucchini, onions,
> cantaloupe, eggplant, and so on**
> **4 cups cider vinegar**
> **2 cups brown sugar**
> **1 tsp. ground cloves**
> **1 tsp. cinnamon**
> **2 tbsp. fresh ginger root**
> **2 cups raisins**

1. Trim any bruised parts off the vegetables and cut them
   into chunks. Take the seeds out of the fruit, but leave the
   peel on the lemons.
2. In a food processor fitted with a chopper blade, chop up
   anything you want chopped fairly fine. To vary the
   texture, cut some of the vegetables by hand.
3. Dump all the vegetables into a large pot (not aluminum or
   cast iron) with a heavy bottom. Add a little water. Bring
   to the boil, then simmer for about an hour.
4. When the vegetables start to get thick and mushy, add the
   vinegar, sugar, cloves, cinnamon, ginger, and raisins.
5. The chutney is ready when it has the texture of runny jam
   and is a nice brown colour. Add more sugar if you wish.

6. Pour into sterilized jars. Seal. Serve with pork, cheese, or curry.

Note: You can use almost anything for this. The whole lemons make a difference to the flavour, and the red and green peppers keep their colour well. The prolific zucchini and green tomatoes make a good base.

Puffy Yorkshire Pudding

Serves 6 to 8
Total time: 1 hour and 30 minutes   **Perri**

I first had this at my friend Margaret's house. It is now a family favourite.

1 cup sifted all-purpose flour
½ tsp. salt
1 cup milk
3 eggs
½ cup drippings from roast or ½ cup vegetable oil

1. Place flour and salt in the bowl of an electric mixer or in a food processor. Turn on the machine and gradually add milk. Add eggs and continue to mix.
2. Chill batter in refrigerator for 20 minutes.
3. Cover the bottom of an 8-inch pan with drippings or oil. Place pan in 425 F oven until pan is sizzling hot.
4. Remove pan. Reduce heat to 375 F. Pour batter into sizzling-hot pan and return to oven. Bake for 40 to 50 minutes. Yorkshire pudding should puff up.
5. To serve, cut in strips.

Note: If you add the milk too quickly, batter will be lumpy.

Beer Beef Stew

Serves 6
Total time: 1 hour and 30 minutes   **Peter**

This is especially good after a party when you have a lot of flat beer around. But be sure to check the old beer bottles for cigarette butts before adding the beer to the stew!

½ cup all-purpose flour
1 tsp. oregano
1 tsp. garlic salt
1 tsp. seasoned salt
1 pound stewing beef, cut into bite-sized pieces
1 tbsp. cooking oil
2 potatoes, peeled, chopped into bite-sized pieces
¼ large turnip, peeled, chopped into bite-sized pieces
2 large carrots, quartered, sliced lengthwise, and cut
    in 3-inch lengths
2 cups water
2 stalks celery, chopped
1 cup green beans
3 cooking onions, quartered
1 cup chopped mushrooms
Dash Worcestershire sauce
Salt and pepper to taste
½ bottle flat beer (fresh is okay)
½ cup fresh parsley

1. In a bowl, combine flour and half the oregano, garlic salt, and seasoned salt.
2. Dust beef with seasoned flour. In a skillet, heat oil. Sauté beef until browned. Set aside.
3. In a stewing pot, put potatoes, turnip, carrots, and water. Bring to a boil.
4. Add beef, celery, beans, onions, and mushrooms. Lower heat to simmer. Add Worcestershire sauce, salt, pepper, and the remaining oregano, garlic salt, and seasoned salt. Cook for 30 minutes.
5. Add the beer and parsley.
6. Simmer for 15 more minutes.
7. Serve with buttered bread.

Note: Veal is a good substitute for the beef.

Leg of Lamb

Serves 6 to 8
Total time: 1 hour   **Janet**

In a tiny restaurant called the Pink Geranium on Galiano Island in British Columbia, our family had lamb that especially impressed us.

1 leg of lamb
2 cloves of garlic, thinly sliced
2 tbsp. fresh ginger root, slivered
Salt and freshly ground pepper
1 tbsp. rosemary

1. With a sharp knife, cut slits in the lamb. With the knife, hold slits open and force the garlic and ginger slices deep into the meat. Rub the lamb with salt, pepper, and rosemary.
2. Roast in a 450 F oven for 20 minutes. Reduce heat to 350 F and roast for 30 to 40 minutes more. The lamb should still be somewhat pink inside.

Note: When cooking a roast, I usually try to put the whole meal in the oven to save energy: roast potatoes, onions, carrots, and eggplant are all good with lamb.

Light and Sublime Lasagna

Serves 6 to 8
Total time: 2 hours

Patsy and Rico

I have had many compliments on my lasagna, and it is a special treat in our family. It requires a lot of time and trouble. The secret is to make lots of meat sauce and freeze it for those times when you want a wonderful entrée. Then all you need to do is make the white sauce and boil the noodles.

Meat sauce:
>   Oil for frying
>   2 onions, minced
>   2 cloves garlic, minced
>   1 carrot, minced
>   2 celery stalks, with leaves
>   ½ pound lean ground beef
>   ¼ pound chicken livers
>   1 8-ounce can tomato paste
>   1 wineglass white wine
>   4 tomatoes, chopped
>   Grating of fresh nutmeg
>   1 tsp. cinnamon
>   Salt and pepper to taste
>   1 tsp. oregano
>   2 bay leaves

White sauce:
>   3 tbsp. butter
>   3 tbsp. all-purpose flour
>   2 cups milk
>   Bay leaf
>   1 tub whipped ricotta cheese
>   ½ tsp. fresh nutmeg, grated
>   Salt and pepper to taste

>   10 or 12 lasagna noodles, dry or fresh
>   ½ cup grated Parmesan cheese

To make the meat sauce:
1. In a large saucepan, heat oil. Sauté onion and garlic. Add carrot and celery. Sauté for 10 more minutes over medium-low heat.
2. Add meat and livers and fry until pinkness is gone.
3. Add tomato paste, wine, tomatoes, nutmeg, cinnamon, salt, pepper, oregano, and bay leaves. Simmer for another 30 minutes.

To make the white sauce:
1. In a saucepan, melt butter. Add flour. Whisk, cooking over medium-low heat for one minute.
2. Add milk slowly, whisking to make sure there are no lumps. Add bay leaf. Cook over low heat until thickened.
3. Add ricotta cheese, nutmeg, salt, and pepper.

To assemble lasagna:
1. Cook lasagna noodles according to package instructions. Remove bay leaf from white sauce.
2. In a 9-by-12-inch casserole, spoon a thin layer of meat sauce. Arrange a layer of lasagna noodles over the meat sauce. Pour white sauce over noodles. Repeat the three steps as many as four times if you have room in the casserole. The final layer of white sauce should be quite thick.
3. Sprinkle casserole with Parmesan cheese.
4. Bake in a 350 F oven for 30 minutes.

Note: Fresh nutmeg is a must. The creamy whipped ricotta makes the white sauce a little different. This is one recipe that is much more fun and less of a hassle if two people make it.

Economical Shepherd's Pie

Serves 4 to 6
Total time: 1 hour **Janet**

This recipe uses the cooked beef heart from Janet's Soup (see page 58). Although much of the flavour has been cooked out, there are still lots of rich nutrients left. A friend of Patsy's copied this recipe out of a copy of *Pierre and Janet Berton's Canadian Food Guide* in the library. It was so successful that she made the recipe the basis for a catering business.

3 tbsp. butter or margarine
1 onion, chopped
3 stalks celery, chopped
1 small cooked beef heart (or 4 cups ground beef,
    lamb, or pork)
½ tsp. marjoram
½ tsp. oregano
½ tsp. thyme
½ tsp. Worcestershire sauce
1 tbsp. all-purpose flour
2 cups mashed potato
Salt and freshly ground pepper to taste

1. In a skillet, melt butter. Sauté onion and celery until transparent.
2. Chop beef heart into small pieces (this can be done in a food processor) and add to sautéd vegetables. Stir (and cook if using raw beef, lamb, or pork). Add marjoram, oregano, thyme, and Worcestershire sauce.
3. In a buttered casserole dish, place meat and vegetables. Sprinkle with flour. (If meat is too dry, moisten with the soup from the heart, or use tomato juice or consommé.)
4. Combine mashed potatoes with salt and pepper. Spread mashed potatoes over meat.
5. Bake in a 350 F oven for 25 minutes.

Baby-Sitter's Spaghetti Casserole ✖

Serves 8 to 10
Total time: 45 minutes   **Janet**

The children always called this dish the baby-sitter's special. It was perfect for those nights – and there were lots of them – when each child had a different schedule of hockey, drama, or ballet classes, or when we left sitters in charge. It's easy to prepare; everyone from babies to teenagers likes it; and it's just as good served immediately or kept warm in the oven.

1 pound hamburger
2 onions, chopped
2 stalks celery, chopped
1 green pepper, chopped
1 28-ounce can tomatoes
Salt and pepper to taste
1 500-g package spaghetti or other pasta
2 tbsp. blue cheese, crumbled (optional)
¼ cup grated cheese

1. In a frying pan, brown meat, stirring until it is light brown and crumbly.
2. Add onions, celery, and green pepper. Cook for 3 minutes.
3. Add tomatoes and simmer for a few minutes. Add salt and pepper.
4. Cook pasta according to package directions; drain.
5. In a buttered 2-quart casserole, combine pasta, sauce, and blue cheese.
6. Sprinkle grated cheese on top. Bake in a 350 F oven for 20 minutes.

Note: A little blue cheese gives this dish a nip.

Barbecued Roast

A woman I met recently said she serves this roast for special occasions and has built an impressive cooking reputation with it. (The recipe was in *Pierre and Janet Berton's Canadian Food Guide*.) Ask your butcher for a rolled porterhouse roast with the tenderloin removed. (Otherwise it will be too unwieldy for the spit.) The roll of meat should weigh about ten pounds. But before the butcher rolls the roast, combine the following herb mixture for the roast.

> 1 tbsp. oregano
> 1 tbsp. thyme
> 1 tbsp. celery seed
> 1 tbsp. marjoram
> 1 tbsp. minced garlic
> ½ tsp. rosemary
> 1 tbsp. cracked black pepper
> 1 tbsp. salt

1 10-pound porterhouse roast, tenderloin removed

1. Take the mixture to your butcher and ask him or her to spread it on the meat and roll it tightly, then cover it with a layer of fat.
2. Place meat on a rotating spit above a hot barbecue for no longer than 45 minutes, if you like your meat rare.
3. To serve, slice with a sharp knife into thick slabs and place either directly on plates or on slices of garlic bread. As a side dish, we usually have a bowlful of fresh spring onions on hand. Nothing else, really, is needed.

Note: There should be enough here to feed ten hungry trenchermen, allowing a pound per person.

VEGETABLES

---MENU---

Vegetable Garden Party

*Corny Soup *by Pierre*

*Summer Salad *by Peter*

*Wonderful Watercress Salad *by Patsy*

*Low-Cal Green-Bean Salad *by Paula*

***Zucchini Bake** *by Janet*

Fresh boiled potatoes with mint *by Penny*

*Peach Shortcake *by Patsy*

Zucchini Bake

Serves 6
Total time: 1 hour   **Janet**

As everyone knows, if you plant one zucchini seed you are likely
to end up with a garden overrun with zucchini. Perhaps because
of this, Pierre says he hates zucchini and won't let it appear on
his table, except for this recipe. It makes a fine luncheon dish,
or a main course for a harvest-time vegetarian dinner.

> **3 or 4 medium-sized zucchini, about 1½ pounds**
> **1 clove garlic**
> **2 cups grated Cheddar cheese**
> **2 eggs, beaten**
> **3 tbsp. all-purpose flour**
> **Pinch nutmeg**
> **1 ounce vermouth**
> **Salt and pepper to taste**
> **¼ cup grated Parmesan cheese**

1. Remove stem and blossom ends from zucchini. Rinse, and
   grate by hand or in a food processor. Add crushed garlic.
   Put into a bowl, sprinkle with salt, and let sit for 15
   minutes. Squeeze out and discard water.
2. In a bowl, combine zucchini, Cheddar cheese, and eggs.
   Stir in flour, nutmeg, vermouth, salt, and pepper.
3. Place mixture in a 1½-quart buttered, shallow casserole.
   Cover with Parmesan cheese. Bake in a 350 F oven for 30
   minutes.

Squash Tofu Pie ✗✗

Serves 4 to 6
Total time: 45 minutes

Penny

Whenever I make this recipe, I think of Japan in autumn, since that's where I first tried it. There was an abundance of tofu and squash. The cheese, however, I often had to do without. Either way, it's delicious with rice and salad.

  2 tbsp. vegetable oil
  1 onion, sliced
  2 cloves garlic, minced
  1 tbsp. ginger, grated
  3 cups boiled mashed squash
  1½ cups tofu, pressed and diced
  1 egg, lightly beaten
  3 tbsp. Tamari soy sauce
  1 tbsp. honey
  1 tsp. cinnamon
  ½ cup raisins (optional)
  ½ cup sesame seeds
  1 cup grated Cheddar cheese

1. In a large, heavy pot or wok, heat oil. Sauté onion, garlic, and ginger until soft.
2. Turn off heat. Add squash, tofu, egg, soy sauce, honey, cinnamon, and raisins. Mix well.
3. Spoon mixture into a well-greased pie pan or shallow baking dish.
4. Sprinkle sesame seeds on top; then sprinkle on cheese. Bake in a 350 F oven for 15 minutes.

Cheese Vegetable Casserole

Serves 2 to 4
Total time: 40 minutes   **Penny**

This is a light and nutritious dish that can be put together in a hurry. It's delicious served with brown rice and a green salad.

2 tbsp. butter
1 onion, chopped
1 clove garlic, crushed
2 tbsp. all-purpose flour
1½ cups milk
1½ cups tofu, mashed
1½ cups grated cheese
½ tsp. nutmeg
1 tsp. dry mustard
1 tsp. savory
¼ cup white wine
3 cups partially steamed broccoli and cauliflower
Salt and freshly ground pepper to taste
¼ cup sesame seeds

1. In a medium-sized saucepan, melt butter. Add onions and garlic, and sauté until soft.
2. Add flour and stir over low heat for 5 minutes.
3. Add milk. Stir with wire whisk constantly until smooth and thick.
4. Add tofu, 1 cup of the cheese, nutmeg, mustard, savory, and wine. Mix well. Add salt and pepper.
5. Place steamed vegetables in a small greased casserole dish. Pour tofu-cheese mixture over them so vegetables are completely immersed. Sprinkle remaining cheese and sesame seeds on top. Bake in a 350 F oven, uncovered, for 15 minutes.

Note: You can vary the vegetables as you like: green beans and zucchini are also good.

Tofu Ginger

Serves 4
Total time: 20 to 25 minutes   **Patsy**

Make this if you're hungry and don't have a lot of time. However, if you don't like hot, spicy food, eliminate the chili or cayenne and cut down on the grated ginger.

   3 tbsp. vegetable oil
   2 onions, minced
   3 cloves garlic, crushed
   2 to 3 tbsp. grated ginger
   ¼ tsp. green chili, chopped fine, or dash cayenne
   2 cakes tofu, diced
   1 to 2 tomatoes, chopped or minced in a food
        processor (optional)
   1 tbsp. water
   1 tbsp. Tamari soy sauce
   1 to 2 tbsp. lemon juice
   Crushed sesame seeds (optional)

1. In a wok or large skillet, heat oil. Fry onion, garlic, ginger, and chili in oil, stirring, for 5 minutes. Add tofu and continue to stir and cook over medium heat.
2. Add tomato and cook for another 10 minutes, stirring frequently. Add water, soy sauce, and lemon juice. Simmer briefly.
3. Sprinkle crushed sesame seeds on top. Serve with brown rice. Eat with chopsticks and think of exotic places.

Note: Steamed broccoli, green pepper, bean sprouts, or carrots can be added. For a nice variation, add creamed coconut.

Eggplant Mushroom Lasagna ✕✕✕

Serves 8 to 10
Total time: 1 hour and 30 minutes **Penny**

This makes a rich and elegant main course for a dinner party.

3 large eggplants, sliced one-half-inch thick
½ cup butter
½ cup all-purpose flour
2½ cups milk
½ fresh nutmeg, grated
Salt and pepper to taste
2 egg yolks
Tomato Mushroom Sauce (see p. 147)
½ pound Mozzarella cheese, coarsely grated
½ cup Parmesan cheese, finely grated

1. Steam eggplant until tender. Drain well.
2. In a small, heavy saucepan, melt butter. Add flour. Stir with a wooden spoon over low heat for 5 minutes.
3. Add milk slowly, stirring constantly with a wire whisk. Add nutmeg, salt, and pepper. Remove from heat.
4. In a small bowl, beat egg yolks. Add a cupful of hot sauce to yolks. Stir constantly with fork until smooth, being careful not to curdle the eggs. Add egg-and-sauce mixture to saucepan.
5. In a well-greased 9-by-14-inch shallow casserole dish, or in two well-greased medium-sized loaf pans, pour a layer of Tomato Mushroom Sauce. Add a layer of eggplant slices, then a layer of mozzarella. Repeat the layers until ingredients are used up.
6. Pour white sauce on top. Cover with a layer of Parmesan cheese. Bake, covered, in a 350 F oven for 30 minutes. Then uncover and bake for 10 more minutes.

Tomato Mushroom Sauce

Serves 6 to 8
Total time: 1 hour   **Penny**

I make this when I'm in the mood to cook, then refrigerate or freeze it. When I'm in a hurry, I use it as a quick spaghetti sauce or a base for casseroles. The flavour definitely improves overnight.

¼ **cup olive oil**
2 tbsp. finely grated ginger
4 cloves garlic, chopped fine
3 large onions, coarsely chopped
1 carrot, chopped
2 28-ounce cans tomatoes
1 6-ounce can tomato paste
2 tbsp. sugar
2 tbsp. chopped parsley
1 tbsp. oregano
1 tbsp. basil
Salt and black pepper to taste
1 cup red wine
1 tsp. cinnamon
1 cake tofu, mashed (optional)
½ pound fresh mushrooms, sliced or dried
**1 cup shiitake mushrooms, soaked in hot water and
    sliced**

1. In a deep cast-iron pot, heat oil. Sauté ginger, garlic, onions, and carrot until onions are soft and transparent.
2. Add tomatoes, tomato paste, and sugar. Mash with potato masher until well blended. Bring to a boil briefly, then reduce heat to simmer.
3. Add parsley, oregano, basil, salt, and pepper. Simmer mixture at least 30 minutes (the longer, the better).
4. Towards the end of cooking, add wine, cinnamon, tofu, and mushrooms. (Fresh mushrooms should be lightly sautéd in butter before they are added.)

Note: The tofu contributes bulk and protein to this meatless sauce. Meat lovers can add 1 pound lean hamburger with the tomatoes.

Dairy-Free Eggplant Casserole ✗✗

Serves 6
Total time: 1 hour **Patsy**

When Liam was born, I developed an allergy to dairy products. This recipe is high in protein but uses no dairy products. It's excellent with noodles or rice on the side.

2 medium eggplants, cut into half-inch rounds
2 cakes tofu, cut in ¼-inch slices
Tomato Mushroom Sauce (see p. 147)
Grated Parmesan cheese (optional)

1. Steam eggplant rounds until tender and soft. Drain for 15 minutes.
2. In a casserole, arrange eggplant in one layer.
3. Place tofu slices over eggplant.
4. Cover with Tomato Mushroom Sauce. Sprinkle with Parmesan.
5. Bake in a 350 F oven until heated through and bubbling hot, about 25 minutes.

Carrot-Mushroom Loaf

Serves 4 to 6
Total time: 1 hour **Penny**

This hearty dish is perfect on a cold, wintry day when your refrigerator is bare except for cheese, eggs, and a bagful of carrots. It is also good served with rice and a green salad.

¼ **cup butter**
2 **cloves garlic, finely chopped**
1 **tbsp. grated ginger**
1 **large onion, chopped**
¼ **tsp. cayenne**
1 **tsp. cumin powder**
1 **tsp. thyme**
4½ **cups grated carrots**
2 **cups shiitake mushrooms, soaked for 5 minutes in**
   hot water and sliced
5 **eggs, lightly beaten**
1 **cup grated Cheddar cheese**
½ **cup whole-wheat breadcrumbs**
½ **cup wheat germ**
½ **cup sesame seeds**
Salt and pepper to taste

1. In a large, heavy saucepan, melt butter. Sauté garlic, ginger, and onion until soft.
2. Add cayenne and cumin and cook a few minutes longer.
3. Add thyme, carrots, mushrooms, eggs, ½ cup of the cheese, and ¼ cup of the breadcrumbs.
4. Spoon mixture into a greased loaf pan. Combine remaining breadcrumbs and cheese with wheat germ, sesame seeds, salt, and pepper. Sprinkle on top of casserole.
5. Cover and bake in a 350 F oven for 30 minutes. Remove cover, and bake for 5 minutes more.

Note: I use dried mushrooms since there are no fresh mushrooms available in Bali. But you can use 1 pound fresh mushrooms; add them to the onion mixture in step 1.

Coconut Cabbage Rolls

Makes 24
Total time: 2 hours and 30 minutes
Penny

Even meat lovers can't always tell the meat is missing in this dish. It's my own Oriental adaptation of the standard Eastern European recipe. The unusual combination of walnuts and tofu has a similar texture to ground beef. Make these ahead of time, put them in the freezer uncooked, and add the coconut cream when you're ready to bake them.

> 1 large green cabbage
> 1½ cups Eggplant Tomato Curry (see p. 154)
> 2 cups cooked brown rice
> ½ cup walnuts, finely chopped
> 1 cake tofu, mashed
> ½ cup raisins
> ¾ cup coconut cream

1. Steam cabbage, stem up, until outer leaves loosen. Cut out core, remove outer leaves gently, and steam the head again. Keep doing this until you've run out of large leaves.
2. In a bowl, mix Eggplant Tomato Curry, rice, walnuts, tofu, and raisins.
3. Fill each cabbage leaf with a heaping spoonful of mixture. Wrap the sides of the leaf in towards the centre, then roll, securing with a toothpick. Place rolls side by side in a large, shallow, oiled baking dish.
4. Mix coconut cream with a little boiling water until smooth. Pour over cabbage rolls. Add more water if necessary (rolls should be covered). Bake, covered, in a 350 F oven for 1 hour.
5. Serve with Yogurt Mint Chutney: Place in a blender 2 cups yogurt, 3 cloves garlic, 1 tbsp. grated ginger, salt to taste, and ½ cup dried mint or 1½ cups fresh mint, packed. Blend until smooth.

Note: Instead of coconut cream, you can make more of the same curry sauce you mixed with the filling; just add water to thin it.

Cumin Chick Peas

Serves 8
Total time: 1 day or overnight **Patsy**

I serve this as an alternative to chili at parties. It can also be made in smaller quantities and served for dinner with rice.

3 cups dry chick peas
6 cups water
Vegetable oil for frying
3 heaping tbsp. grated ginger
6 large cloves garlic, minced
4 large onions, chopped
3 tsp. cumin powder, or more to taste
2 tbsp. cumin seeds
1 tsp. mustard seeds
1 tsp. turmeric
3 tsp. coriander
Bay leaf
2 tsp. curry powder, or more to taste
Cayenne to taste
4 stalks celery, chopped
1 green pepper, chopped
1 28-ounce can tomatoes
3 carrots, diced
1 cup unsweetened coconut (optional)
Lemon juice to taste

1. In a large saucepan, soak chick peas in water for 1 hour. Then boil until tender, about 1½ hours.
2. In a large saucepan, heat oil. Sauté ginger, garlic, onions, cumin powder and seeds, mustard seeds, turmeric, coriander, bay leaf, curry powder, and cayenne for 10 minutes over medium-low heat.
3. Add cooked chick peas, celery, green pepper, tomatoes, carrots, coconut, and lemon juice.
4. Place in casserole and bake in a 350 F oven for several hours until most of liquid has been absorbed, but the casserole is still quite juicy.

Klondike Baked Beans

Serves 8 to 10
Total time: Overnight   **Pierre**

This hearty meal improves with age. It freezes easily, and can be kept in the fridge for several days. Without beans, there would have been no Klondike gold rush. We made a version of this when the family floated down the Yukon River, and it was good for three days.

    1 pound navy beans
    2 bay leaves, crushed
    ½ cup finely chopped parsley
    2 cloves garlic, crushed
    1 tbsp. oregano
    ½ pound salt pork, cut in large cubes
    4 large tomatoes
    1 6-ounce can tomato paste
    4 large onions, chopped
    1 tbsp. dry English mustard
    1 tbsp. Worcestershire sauce
    1 tbsp. celery seed
    1 cup molasses
    1 cup sherry or rum

1. Soak the beans overnight in cold water to cover.
2. In a large pan, place soaked beans, bay leaves, parsley, garlic, and oregano. Cover with water. Simmer for one hour. Drain, reserving the liquid. Set beans aside.
3. Return liquid to pan. Add tomatoes, tomato paste, onions, mustard, Worcestershire sauce, and celery seed. Simmer for 30 minutes, then stir in molasses.
4. Place reserved beans in a large casserole. Add pork cubes, then pour tomato sauce over casserole.
5. Bake in a 250 F oven for 4 hours. Add sherry or rum 15 minutes before serving.

Dahl (Lentil Soup)

Serves 4 to 6
Total time: 2 to 3 hours   **Patsy**

After five months in India, Rico and I learned to love dahl, a hot and spicy bean soup. With rice and salad, it makes a satisfying but light dinner.

> 1 cup dry mung beans
> 4 cups water
> 3 tbsp. vegetable oil
> 2 onions, minced
> 3 cloves garlic
> 2 tbsp. grated ginger
> 1 to 2 tsp. whole cumin
> 1 tsp. powdered cumin
> 3 tsp. powdered coriander
> 1 tsp. black mustard seed
> Pinch of cayenne (to taste), or 1 tsp. fresh chili, chopped
> 2 stalks celery, chopped fine
> 2 carrots, grated
> 1 28-ounce can tomatoes (optional)
> 2 to 3 tbsp. lemon juice (to taste)
> Salt to taste

1. Soak mung beans in water for 1 to 2 hours. Rinse. Boil in water until beans are tender. Set aside.
2. In a heavy saucepan, heat oil. Sauté onions, garlic, and ginger for 5 minutes. Add whole and powdered cumin, coriander, mustard seed, and cayenne or chili.
3. When mustard begins to pop, turn heat down and add celery, carrots, and tomatoes. Cook until vegetables are tender.
4. Add cooked beans and more water if needed to make soup. Add lemon juice and salt to taste. Heat and serve as soup or with rice.

Eggplant Tomato Curry

Serves 4 to 6
Total time: 45 minutes **Penny**

This is a versatile recipe. Multiply the ingredients and it is an easy and inexpensive way to feed a lot of people. Make it a day ahead and you'll find it is even better the next day. Eliminate the eggplant and it makes a good basic curry sauce, to which you can add any combination of steamed vegetables you like.

¼ cup vegetable oil
3 large onions, chopped
2 tbsp. finely grated ginger
4 cloves garlic, minced
1 tsp. cumin powder
1 tsp. coriander powder
1 tsp. turmeric
1 tsp. Garam Masala (available at Indian food stores)
1 tsp. cayenne or 1 chili, minced
1 28-ounce can tomatoes
2 medium eggplants, diced
Salt to taste
½ cup plain yogurt (optional)

1. In a large, deep saucepan or wok, heat oil. Sauté onions, ginger, and garlic until onions are transparent.
2. Add cumin powder, coriander powder, turmeric, Garam Masala, and cayenne or chili. Sauté over low heat for about 5 minutes, stirring occasionally.
3. Add tomatoes and diced eggplant. Bring to a boil, then lower heat and continue to cook, stirring occasionally, until vegetables become soft and mushy. Add about ½ cup water if the mixture sticks to the pan.
4. Add salt to taste and yogurt. Serve with rice.

Scalloped Potatoes with Cheese

Serves 8
Total time: 1 hour and 30 minutes   **Janet**

This recipe is a distinct improvement on many old-fashioned recipes that call for potatoes, milk, and onions. Served with home-smoked ham, this dish makes an excellent buffet supper for a large evening party.

8 potatoes
Salt and pepper to taste
½ pound Gruyère cheese, thinly sliced
Dijon mustard
8 onions, thinly sliced
½ pound Canadian Cheddar cheese, thinly sliced or
    crumbled
1 cup dry white wine or chicken stock or pale
    vegetable juices
½ cup fine breadcrumbs
½ cup grated Parmesan cheese
½ cup butter

1. Slice potatoes thinly. Place a layer of them in a well-buttered baking dish.
2. Sprinkle with salt and pepper and cover with a layer of Gruyère.
3. Spread mustard over the Gruyère. Top with a layer of the onions.
4. Repeat these layers until the dish is full, alternating the layers of Gruyère with layers of Cheddar.
5. Press the layers down firmly and cover with the wine.
6. Sprinkle the entire dish with breadcrumbs and Parmesan cheese and dot with butter. Cover with buttered waxed paper.
7. Bake in a 350 F oven for 1 hour. Remove the cover, brown the top and serve very hot.

Sesame Green Beans

Serves 4 to 6
Total time: 40 minutes   **Patsy**

This recipe was one of my first experiments with ginger and garlic, and it gave me a whole new appreciation of vegetables. I started learning from my friend Ann Clifford when I was fifteen, at a community school where we fed at least forty people at each meal. This recipe can be adapted to feed just as many – and it's also good cold for pot lucks.

> **4 cups green beans**
> **2 to 3 tbsp. vegetable oil**
> **2 garlic cloves, minced or crushed**
> **1 tbsp. grated ginger**
> **1 onion, sliced lengthwise**
> **2 tbsp. Tamari soy sauce**
> **¼ cup toasted whole sesame seeds**
> **Squeeze of lemon (optional)**

1. Remove stems from green beans and cut in half crosswise. Steam cut green beans until just tender and still bright green.
2. In a wok or large skillet, heat oil. Sauté garlic, ginger, and onion over medium-low heat for 5 to 10 minutes.
3. Add green beans and soy sauce. Add an inch of water to thin the soy sauce, then cover and cook for 1 minute. Add sesame seeds and lemon juice. Stir. Serve hot or cold.

Green Beans with Cashews

Serves 2 to 4
Total time: 30 minutes   **Penny and John**

When we first travelled in Indonesia, we mostly ate in little food stalls run by families. After a while, we got tired of eating the same thing every day, so we'd go into the restaurant kitchen and get involved. This is one of the results.

½ **lb. green beans**
½ **cup chopped raw cashews**
1 tbsp. oil (sesame oil is especially tasty)
2 tbsp. butter (unsalted)
1 or 2 large cloves garlic, chopped
1 tsp. finely grated ginger
1 small chili, finely chopped, or ½ tsp. cayenne
    powder (optional)
1 tbsp. Tamari soy sauce

1. Remove stems from beans and cut in half diagonally. Steam until a fork easily penetrates the beans (about 7 to 10 minutes), but before they lose their bright green colour.
2. Meanwhile, fry cashews in a little oil, or toast in a heavy wok without oil, until they are golden brown. Remove from heat.
3. In a heavy wok, heat oil and butter. Sauté garlic, ginger, and chili or cayenne briefly over low heat.
4. Add beans. Mix well until beans are well coated with the sauce.
5. Add soy sauce and mix well. Add cashews and serve immediately.

Better Broccoli

Serves 6
Total time: 10 minutes **Penny**

I have to sneak broccoli into the Kleinburg kitchen since Dad has given strict orders that it not be allowed on the table. I suspect that during his childhood, he was terrified by a piece of broccoli that had been boiled until it was grey. Maybe if he tries this recipe, he'll change his mind.

> **1 large or 2 small bunches of broccoli, cut into flowerets**
> **2 tbsp. butter**
> **1 clove garlic, minced**
> **1 tsp. finely grated ginger**
> **¼ cup Tamari soy sauce**
> **Juice of ½ lemon**

1. Steam broccoli for about 7 minutes, or until tender to a fork. (If the green colour has faded, it's overcooked.) Rinse in cold water to stop cooking.
2. In small saucepan, heat butter. Sauté garlic and ginger over low heat; add soy sauce and lemon. Heat through.
3. Pour sauce over broccoli and toss lightly; serve immediately. Or you can put the sauce in a small jug and serve separately at the table.

Note: This is a delicious sauce for any freshly steamed green vegetable, especially green beans.

Saffron Sesame Rice

Serves 8 to 12
Total time: 45 minutes **John**

This delicately spiced rice is Elora's favourite meal. It is delicious all on its own, and goes well with a main dish that doesn't include a sauce.

4 cups brown rice (short-grain rice is best)
4 cups water
**1 tbsp. Garam Masala (available at Indian food
    stores)**
½ tsp. cayenne
Pinch saffron
Salt to taste
1 cup sesame seeds

1. Wash rice until water runs clear. Drain.
2. In an electric rice cooker, combine rice and water. Add Garam Masala, cayenne, saffron, and salt. Cook rice. (If you don't have a rice cooker, use a saucepan with a tight-fitting lid. Add rice and seasonings to 6 cups salted boiling water. Cover and cook over low heat for 30 to 40 minutes, or until all the water has been absorbed.)
3. Meanwhile, toast sesame seeds in a dry skillet. Then partially grind in a food processor.
4. Add sesame seeds to cooked rice, and serve in a heated dish.

Squash Yogurt   ✕

Serves 4 to 6
Total time: 30 minutes   **Patsy**

This pretty side dish has an appealing sweet-sour flavour.

1 acorn squash, peeled and cubed
½ cup yogurt, or more to taste
1 tbsp. fresh dill or 1 tbsp. dill seed
1 clove garlic
Sprig of parsley

1. Steam squash until tender. Put hot squash in blender and blend until smooth.
2. Add yogurt, dill, and garlic. Blend till smooth.
3. Garnish with parsley and serve immediately.

Pesto Sauce

Makes 3 cups
Total time: 20 minutes **Pamela**

When I first made this fragrant green sauce for pasta, Peter and Dad said they wouldn't eat it because of the colour. Now I can't make enough. Make it in large quantities and you'll always have something to serve for emergency suppers.

>**2 cups fresh basil leaves, washed and dried**
>**5 large cloves garlic**
>**½ to 1 cup olive oil**
>**¼ cup pine nuts**
>**1 cup grated Parmesan cheese**

1. In a blender or food processor, place basil and garlic; add a little oil to lubricate. Blend.
2. While still processing, add pine nuts, then cheese. Add more oil. The mixture should have the texture of thick applesauce.
3. To serve, spoon a small amount over hot linguine or spaghetti. Toss to coat pasta.
4. To store, place in sterilized jars and pour a film of oil on the top. Seal. I keep it in the fridge like this all winter. I know people who freeze it, but I don't like the texture.

Note: If you're on a budget, substitute walnuts for the pine nuts. They taste almost the same.

Tahini Tofu Sauce

Serves 4
Total time: 15 minutes **Patsy and Rico**

For years, we have searched for the perfect falafels, in restaurants all over the world. We've decided that the most important ingredient is the tahini sauce. Here's an interesting variation. The addition of tofu makes this a great sauce for steamed vegetables, particularly eggplant.

1½ cups tahini
2 cups buttermilk
1 or 2 cloves garlic
½ cup lemon juice
¼ cup minced parsley
1 tsp. cumin powder
Pinch cayenne
½ to 1 cake tofu (optional)

1. Put all ingredients in blender, and blend until smooth.

Oriental Sauce for Steamed Vegetables

Serves 4 to 6
Total time: 10 minutes   **Patsy and Penny**

This is great to have on hand. Keep it in the fridge and use it, hot or cold, as needed. It is good with steamed vegetables or fish fillets.

½ cup Tamari soy sauce
½ cup water
¼ cup lemon juice
2 tbsp. grated ginger
2 tbsp. crushed garlic
¼ cup oil

1. Mix all ingredients together in a jar.

Fantasy Food

Serves any number
Total time: 20 minutes **Penny and Elora**

Like most kids, Elora is often picky when it comes to eating
certain vegetables. One day, I came up with an inspiration: it's
all in the presentation! Now she gobbles up her "broccoli trees"
as fast as I can get them on her plate. Here are some ideas we've
come up with together:

Broccoli, cut into flowerets
Cauliflower, cut into flowerets
Asparagus tips
Carrot, sliced crosswise
Celery, cut into thin sticks
Alfalfa sprouts
1 hard-boiled egg
Slice of tomato, halved

1. Steam broccoli, cauliflower, asparagus, and carrot lightly.
2. On a plate, arrange "broccoli trees," "asparagus pine
   trees," and "cauliflower clouds" like a painting. Add alfalfa
   sprouts for "grass."
3. Place a celery stick crosswise and arrange the carrots as
   wheels to make a "carrotmobile." Use a slice of tomato for
   the body of the car.
4. Add a slice of hard-boiled egg for the "sun," or a crescent
   of egg white for the "moon."

Note: You can create other scenes together with your
   children, using your combined imaginations to expand on
   these ideas.

DESSERTS

Oriental Anniversary Dinner

*Spicy Crab Snacks *by Peter*

*Apple-Curry Soup *by Penny*

*Korean Grocer's Salad *by Peggy Anne*

*Wounded Pickerel *by Paul*

Rice *by Eric*

*Sesame Green Beans *by Patsy*

***Grand Marnier Soufflé** by Pamela*

***Deadly Chocolate-Chip Cookies** by Perri*

Grand Marnier Soufflé

Makes 1 6-cup soufflé
Total time: 1 hour **Pamela**

In our house, this is the ultimate in elegance. It is also Dad's favourite decadent dessert. Besides being too fattening, it is too much effort to make very often. It helps if you are organized beforehand and can keep your guests from wandering away during the hiatus before dessert, since it must be served immediately.

5 egg yolks
¼ cup sugar
3 tbsp. all-purpose flour
1 cup boiling milk
1 tsp. vanilla
Zest of 1 orange
¼ cup Grand Marnier liqueur
5 egg whites
¼ tsp. cream of tartar
**6-cup soufflé dish, buttered and sprinkled with 2 tbsp.
    white sugar**

Before dinner:
1. Mix egg yolks and sugar together in a bowl. Blend in flour.
2. Add boiling milk. Blend and transfer mixture to the top of a double boiler.
3. Fill the bottom of the double boiler with water, and bring it to a boil.
4. Place top of double boiler with egg mixture over direct heat. Stir until egg mixture boils and thickens.
5. Remove from heat and continue stirring for another minute, then add vanilla, zest, and Grand Marnier. Place the top of the double boiler over the hot water. Cover with a lid to keep warm.

After dinner:
1. Preheat oven to 425 F. Beat egg whites until foamy. Add cream of tartar and continue to beat until stiff.
2. Mix a little of the egg whites into the custard in the double boiler to lighten it, then gently fold in remaining egg whites.

3. Pour carefully into prepared dish. Place in oven and reduce heat to 375 F. Bake for 20 minutes for a soft soufflé, 30 minutes for one that is more solid.

Deadly Chocolate-Chip Cookies ✖✖

Makes 48
Total time: 1 hour **Perri**

I have tried a lot of chocolate-chip-cookie recipes, but I was never satisfied, even though the cookies always got eaten. This one is the result of years of experimenting.

1 cup butter or margarine
¼ cup sugar
1 cup brown sugar
2 eggs
1 tbsp. milk
1 tsp. vanilla
1½ cups all-purpose flour
1 tsp. baking soda
1 tsp. cinnamon
½ tsp. salt
Rind of 1 orange
Rind of 1 lemon
2 cups quick-cooking oatmeal
2 cups chocolate chips

1. Cream butter and sugars.
2. Add eggs, milk, and vanilla.
3. Sift together flour, soda, cinnamon, and salt. Add to butter and egg mixture. Add orange and lemon rind. Mix well.
4. Stir in oatmeal and chocolate chips.
5. Drop by medium-sized spoonfuls on a greased cookie sheet.
6. Bake in a 375 F oven for 10 to 12 minutes, or until brown.
Note: You can use more white sugar and less brown, if you wish. The more brown sugar you use, the chewier the cookie.

Lemon Jelly

Serves 8
Total time: 2 hours **Janet**

People who have trouble making jelly can't miss with this one. Pierre's favourite, it is a light dessert, especially refreshing after a rich or heavy meal.

> ¼ **cup cold water**
> 2 **packages (or 2 tbsp.) unflavoured gelatin**
> 1 **cup boiling water**
> ¾ **cup sugar, or 11 packages dry "Equal" sugar sub-**
> **stitute**
> 1 **cup lemon juice, preferably fresh**
> **Ice cubes**
> 1 **tbsp. grated lemon rind**

1. In a 4-cup Pyrex measuring cup (this makes the recipe foolproof), put ¼ cup cold water. Sprinkle gelatin over it until softened.
2. Add boiling water to dissolve gelatin, then add sugar and stir until dissolved. Add lemon juice.
3. Fill the 4-cup measuring cup to the top with ice cubes. Stir until the ice cubes partly melt and the mixture has the consistency of unbeaten egg whites.
4. Remove any unmelted ice cubes. Fold in lemon rind.
5. Place in the fridge for 5 or 10 minutes. Or transfer to a mould that has been rinsed with cold water and refrigerate. When set, jelly may be unmoulded: dip the mould for a few seconds into a large bowl of warm water – not too hot or the whole thing will melt away – and turn out on a plate. Serve alone or with whipped cream.

Note: Frozen, unsweetened raspberries or strawberries may be added (and the jelly can be put in the blender, if desired), but the lemon juice is still necessary to give the dish a little more flavour. The main thing is to have the whole mixture fill exactly the 4-cup measuring cup.

Lemon Snow

When Lemon Jelly is partly set, beat with an egg beater and add the beaten whites of 2 eggs.

Ruby-Red Raspberry Mousse

Serves 6 to 8
Total time: 10 minutes **Janet**

This is not at all like Lemon Snow. It is much heavier because of the whipped cream, but it is a beautiful finale to a meal.

    ¼ cup cold water
    2 pkg. unsweetened, unflavoured gelatin
    1 cup boiling water
    ⅔ cup sugar
    1 pkg. frozen raspberries, unsweetened
    ¼ cup lemon juice
    Grated rind of one lemon
    1 cup whipping cream

1. In a 4-cup Pyrex measuring cup, put the cold water. Sprinkle the gelatin over it until softened.
2. Add boiling water and stir to dissolve. Add sugar and stir to dissolve.
3. Add frozen raspberries. Stir.
4. Put in blender. Blend for one minute. Return to measuring cup and refrigerate.
5. In a bowl, whip cream. When gelatin is partly set, fold in cream.
6. Pour into mould rinsed with cold water. Put in refrigerator to set (it will take only a few minutes because the raspberries are so cold). Unmould by dipping the mould in a large dish of warm (not hot) water, and turning out on a plate.

Note: Practically any fruit may be used. Strawberries and blueberries need a little more lemon juice. The main thing to remember is to use a 4-cup measuring cup. As long as the mixture fits into the cup before folding in the cream, the 2 pkg. of gelatin will set that amount. Beaten egg whites may be used instead of whipping cream. Then it's Raspberry Snow.

Cobanalot Cake

Serves 4 to 6 (with seconds)
Total time: 1 hour and 20 minutes **Paula**

I remember the first time I brought a homemade cake out to the family in Kleinburg as a gift. I was in a hurry and rushed to the car with the cake still warm from the oven. As it sat in my lap during the drive, it slowly caved in and became a natural disaster. With a lump in my throat, I presented it to Janet. She instantly perceived my distress, whipped up some cream, dabbed it on, and saved my cake – and my ego. A friend helped devise the name of this cake recipe – a combination of coconut, banana, and chocolate – after consuming several pieces.

¾ **cup milk**
1 **cup mashed banana (about 2 bananas)**
1 **tsp. baking soda**
1 **cup butter, softened**
1 **cup sugar**
2 **eggs, beaten**
1 **tsp. vanilla**
1½ **cups all-purpose flour**
½ **tsp. salt**
½ **cup chocolate chips**
1 **tbsp. grated coconut**

Topping:
½ **cup brown sugar**
¼ **cup chopped walnuts**
½ **cup chocolate chips**
½ **cup coconut**

1. In a bowl, mix milk, banana, and baking soda. Set aside.
2. In another bowl, cream together butter and sugar. Add eggs, vanilla, and banana mixture. Mix well.
3. In a third bowl, sift together flour and salt. Add the banana batter. Mix well.
4. Gently stir in chocolate chips.
5. Grease an 8-inch square pan and cover bottom with the grated coconut.

6. Pour in batter.
7. To make topping: combine brown sugar, walnuts, and chocolate chips. Cover cake with topping. Sprinkle coconut on top.
8. Bake in a 350 F oven for 45 to 50 minutes, or until topping is brown and fork comes out clean.

Canadjan, Eh? Butter Tarts

Makes 18
Total time: 1 hour   **Pamela**

Butter tarts, that staple of church-basement bake sales and pot-luck teas, don't exist in the rest of the world. They do, however, travel well. Margaret Bodsworth always makes them for our birding trip to Point Pelee in the spring. The non-birders in the family are beginning to suspect we go for the tarts instead of the birds. My version tends to the non-runny end of the butter-tart scale.

    ¼ **cup soft butter**
    ½ **cup brown sugar**
    ¼ **cup maple syrup**
    ½ **tbsp. grated lemon rind**
    1 **cup raisins**
    ½ **cup walnut pieces**
    Pastry for 1 large pie shell (see p. 186), rolled and cut to fit tart pans

1. In a food processor or electric mixer, cream butter and sugar.
2. Add maple syrup and lemon rind. Mix well. Stir in raisins and walnuts.
3. Spoon into prepared tart shells. Fill each shell about two-thirds full.
4. Bake in a 375 F oven about 25 minutes, or until the filling foams.

"Hardy" Christmas Cake

Makes 3 cakes
Total time: 4 to 5 hours

John

When I was a kid, I used to help my mother, Esther Hardy, mix the heavy batter for her favourite Christmas cake. Now that I'm rarely home at Christmas time, she mails us samples of cake to Bali in tape-cassette containers.

2 cups butter
3 cups sugar
12 eggs
4 cups currants
4 cups sultana raisins
4 cups seeded raisins
1 cup dates
1 cup mixed peel
1 cup citron peel
1 cup candied fruit, mixed
6 fruit rings
2 cups candied cherries, red and green
1½ cups almonds
1 cup grape juice or brandy
½ cup molasses
1 tsp. vanilla
3½ cups all-purpose flour
1 tsp. salt
1 tsp. baking soda
¼ tsp. mace
¼ tsp. nutmeg
¼ tsp. cinnamon
¼ tsp. allspice

1. In a very large bowl, cream the butter until smooth. Add sugar gradually. Add the eggs one at a time. Mix well.
2. In another bowl, combine currants, raisins, dates, peel, mixed fruit, fruit rings, cherries, and almonds. Pour fruit juice, molasses, and vanilla on top. Mix well.

3. In a small bowl, sift together flour, salt, soda, mace, nutmeg, cinnamon, and allspice.
4. Add flour mixture to creamed mixture. Mix well.
5. Add fruit mixture. Stir well. You may need more than one person for this.
6. Line three 9-inch cake tins with heavy brown paper. Fill three-quarters full with batter.
7. Bake in a 275 F oven for 3 hours and 15 minutes, or until a toothpick comes out clean.

Spring Rhubarb Pie

Makes 1 9-inch pie
Total time: 1 hour   **Perri**

This is the first fresh pie of spring, since rhubarb is always the first sign of spring to appear in the garden.

Pastry for 9-inch pie shell (see p. 186)
3 tbsp. all-purpose flour
1 tsp. cinnamon
1 cup sugar
2 eggs, beaten
Rind of 1 lemon
Rind of 1 orange
3 cups rhubarb, cut into half-inch pieces

1. Line a 9-inch pie plate with pastry.
2. In a large bowl, mix flour, cinnamon, sugar, eggs, and lemon and orange rind.
3. Add rhubarb and mix.
4. Pour into pastry-lined pie dish.
5. Cover with full top or lattice top.
6. Bake pie in a 450 F oven for 10 minutes. Lower heat to 350 F and bake for 30 minutes, or until pie is set. Serve with vanilla ice cream.

Orange Pumpkin Pie

Makes 1 9-inch pie
Total time: 1 hour and 30 minutes   **Perri**

I found this recipe in the Toronto *Star* years ago. They phoned recently to ask what our favourite pumpkin pie was, and we told them about this one.

Pastry for 9-inch pie shell (see p. 186)
⅔ **cup brown sugar**
1½ **tsp. cinnamon**
½ **tsp. ginger**
¼ **tsp. nutmeg**
½ **tsp. salt**
Grated rind of 1 orange
2 eggs, slightly beaten
1¼ **cups canned pumpkin, or fresh pumpkin, cooked
    then sieved**
1 cup milk
⅓ **cup orange juice (fresh or frozen)**
¼ **cup water**
1 tsp. vanilla

1. Line a 9-inch pie plate with pastry.
2. Mix together sugar, cinnamon, ginger, nutmeg, salt, and orange rind. Add eggs. Mix well.
3. Stir in pumpkin, milk, orange juice, water, and vanilla.
4. Pour batter into pie shell.
5. Bake in 425 F oven for 10 minutes. Reduce heat to 325 F. Bake for 40 minutes more, or until filling is almost set.

Sultry Tarts

Makes about 36 bite-sized tarts
Total time: 2 hours

Paula

This recipe comes from my granny, May Forrester, who did not like cooking. But, boy, could she bake! These are perfect for bake sales.

Pastry:
> 1 cup shortening
> 2 cups all-purpose flour
> 1 egg yolk
> 1 tsp. vinegar
> Cold water

Lemon Curd:
> ½ cup butter
> 2 cups sugar
> 6 eggs
> Juice of 3 lemons
> 1 cup whipping cream (optional)

To make pastry:
1. Cut together shortening and flour.
2. In a measuring cup, put egg yolk, vinegar, and enough cold water to make ½ cup of liquid.
3. Add egg mixture to flour mixture. Blend to moisten, then wrap in a plastic bag. Chill.
4. Roll out to about ¼-inch thickness. Don't roll it too thin. Cut with glass or cookie cutter to size of tart cups.
5. Press into tart cups with fingers. Bake in a 350 F oven for 10 to 15 minutes (longer for larger tarts), until lightly browned.

To make curd:
1. In the top of a double boiler, combine butter, sugar, eggs, and lemon juice. Cook, stirring constantly, over hot water until mixture coats back of spoon, about 20 minutes.
2. Cool and spoon into cooked shells. If desired, whip cream and place a dollop on each tart before serving.

Chocolate Cake

Makes 2 9-inch square or round cakes
Total time: 50 minutes

Janet

I found this recipe in a magazine ad for Cow Brand baking soda just after the war. Many recipes at that time had been redesigned to use fewer eggs and less butter. This is easy to make and economical, and for years it has been the standby with us for the children's birthday cakes.

> **3 cups sifted all-purpose flour**
> **2 tsp. baking soda**
> **½ tsp. salt**
> **2 cups sugar**
> **2 cups sour milk (To make 1 cup sour milk: put 1 tbsp. lemon juice or vinegar in a 1-cup measuring cup. Fill with milk and stir.)**
> **2 eggs, well-beaten**
> **4 squares unsweetened chocolate, melted**
> **4 tsp. melted butter**
> **2 tsp. vanilla**

1. Sift together flour, soda, and salt.
2. In a large bowl dissolve sugar in soured milk. Add eggs.
3. Blend in chocolate and melted butter.
4. Add dry ingredients to mixture in batches. Beat after each addition. Add vanilla.
5. Pour into 2 9-inch cake pans. Bake in a 350 F oven for 25 minutes, or until toothpick inserted in centre comes out clean. Cool on racks. Ice with chocolate or vanilla icing.

Pots de Chocolate (Chocolate Mousse-Maker's Revenge)

Serves 8
Total time: 5 minutes and 1 hour to chill   **Patsy**

This recipe is a godsend to all the chocolate-mousse makers who have failed miserably. It also keeps for days and has even been known to be eaten before lunch.

> **2 cups chocolate chips (real chocolate, not chocolate-flavoured)**
> **3 eggs**
> **3 tbsp. brandy, Cointreau, or orange liqueur**
> **2 tsp. orange rind**
> **1 cup boiling milk**

1. Place chocolate chips, eggs, brandy, and orange rind in a blender. Add boiling milk.
2. Blend for 3 minutes or until smooth. Pour into little pots or ramekins.
3. Chill at least an hour.

Peach Shortcake

Serves 12
Total time: 1 hour   **Patsy**

This is a wonderful way to eat peaches.

Peaches:
  18 peaches, peeled and sliced
  2 tbsp. sugar
  2 tbsp. lemon juice

Shortcake:
  1 cup unbleached white flour
  2 tsp. baking powder
  ½ tsp. baking soda
  1 tbsp. sugar
  ¾ tsp. salt
  1 cup whole-wheat flour
  ⅓ cup butter or margarine
  1 cup buttermilk

Whipped cream:
  2 cups whipping cream
  1 tsp. vanilla
  3 tsp. sugar

1. In a large bowl, combine peach slices with sugar and lemon juice. Transfer half the peaches to another bowl and mash lightly.
2. To make shortcake: Sift together white flour, baking powder, soda, sugar, and salt.
3. Add whole-wheat flour and mix well.
4. Cut in butter with pastry cutter until mixture has the consistency of fine crumbs.
5. Add buttermilk all at once, stirring with a fork. Turn out onto floured board and roll until one inch thick.
6. Cut into rounds and place on ungreased cookie sheet. Make sure the rounds touch each other. Bake in a 400 F oven for 12 to 15 minutes, until light brown. (The rounds on the outside will be crusty.)

7. Whip cream with vanilla and sugar until stiff.
8. When biscuits are cool, slice each in half horizontally. Top with a dollop of whipped cream and a spoonful of mashed peaches. Add top of biscuit. Cover with sliced peaches.

Note: Strawberries can be used instead of peaches.

Rico's Rice Pudding   �✖

Serves 8 to 12
Total time: 1 hour and 20 minutes   **Rico**

This recipe is of mammoth proportions because I love to eat it. The trick is not to use too much rice but still maintain maximum volume. If it looks dry, add another egg or more milk.

2 cups milk
4 eggs
4 cups cooked long-grain brown rice
½ tsp. salt
½ cup brown sugar
1 tsp. vanilla
1½ tbsp. grated orange rind
Juice of 1 orange
¾ cup raisins
¼ tsp. fresh grated nutmeg
Pinch of cinnamon

1. In a large bowl, combine milk and eggs. Mix well. Add rice and mix with a fork until smooth.
2. Add the remaining ingredients. Mix well. Pour into a large greased baking dish.
3. Sprinkle more cinnamon on top. Bake in a 325 F oven about 50 minutes or until pudding is set. Be careful not to overcook. After 50 minutes the pudding may seem uncooked or runny in the middle, but it will set in the fridge. It can be served hot or cold.

Old English Trifle

Serves 20
Total time: 45 minutes   **Janet**

There are many versions of this dish, such as "Tipsy Cake," but this is our favourite one because we are convinced that any really good trifle must be loaded with liquor.

Custard:
    6 egg yolks
    ½ cup sugar
    1 lemon rind, grated
    ¼ tsp. salt
    2 cups milk, scalded
    2 ounces brandy
    ½ tsp. vanilla extract

Trifle:
    1 sponge cake
    ½ cup sherry or Madeira wine
    **1 14-ounce package frozen raspberries, thawed and
        drained**
    **1 20-ounce can unsweetened pineapple chunks,
        drained**
    1 cup whipping cream
    ½ cup sugar
    Brandy (optional)
    Candied cherries for garnish
    Slivered almonds for garnish

1. To make custard, in the top of a double boiler combine egg yolks, sugar, lemon rind, and salt.
2. Add scalded milk slowly to the egg mixture in the top of a double boiler. Cook custard over hot water, stirring all the time, until it coats a spoon.
3. Cool and add the brandy and vanilla extract.
4. Cut sponge cake into finger-sized pieces. Lay a few pieces of cake in the bottom of a glass bowl (a glass bowl is preferable so that you can see the various layers).
5. Drizzle a little sherry over cake. Cover with the raspberries.

6. Add a layer of custard and another layer of cake and more sherry; then cover with the pineapple.
7. Top with the rest of the custard, letting it dribble right down to the bottom.
8. Whip cream with the ½ cup of sugar and more brandy if desired, and top the trifle with it. Decorate with small pieces of candied cherries and slivered almonds. This dish can be the pièce de résistance of a successful buffet for a party of 20.

Bananas Flambé

Serves 4 to 6
Total time: 20 minutes **Janet**

An impressive but simple finale to any meal. It can easily be put together at the last minute.

4 bananas
¼ cup brown sugar
¼ cup lemon juice
2 tsp. grated lemon rind
¼ cup shredded coconut (optional)
½ cup Demerara rum

1. Peel the bananas and split them in half lengthwise. Place them in a well-buttered oblong baking dish (choose one you're prepared to put on the table).
2. Sprinkle the sugar, lemon juice, lemon rind, coconut, and half the rum over the fruit. Bake in a 450 F oven for 10 minutes, or until the bananas are tender, basting them at least twice. Remove from the oven.
3. Heat the rest of the rum in a small dish. Pour it over the bananas and set it alight. Serve while flaming.
Note: This can also be made in a chafing dish at the table.

Zabaglione

Serves 6
Total time: 25 minutes **Pamela**

Since this rich dessert is best served immediately, I make it between courses at dinner parties when people enjoy a rest anyway. It means leaving your guests alone, but it's worth the effort.

8 egg yolks
⅔ cup sugar
¾ cup dry white wine
¼ cup Triple Sec or orange liqueur
1 14-ounce package frozen raspberries

1. Before you sit down to the main course, in the top of a double boiler, mix egg yolks and sugar. Measure out wine and liqueur, and set out a whisk.
2. When you are ready for dessert, beat egg mixture over hot water until it is foamy and starts to thicken.
3. Add wine and liqueur and continue to beat over the hot water until the custard thickens again.
4. Place frozen raspberries in glass bowls or sherbet glasses. Pour hot sauce over raspberries and serve immediately.

Note: You can whip the leftover egg whites into "clouds" to serve with the zabiglione, or cook them into meringues.

Raspberry Meringues

Serves 10
Total time: 3 hours

Pierre and Janet

This recipe solves the problem of what to do with the egg whites left over from the turkey paste (see pages 116-119). After the richness of the turkey, these meringues make an excellent light dessert. Some people prefer them to a heavy plum pudding on Christmas Day.

8 egg whites
2 tsp. vinegar
4 tsp. vanilla
2 cups white sugar
4 cups fresh or frozen raspberries
½ cup kirschwasser

1. In a bowl, combine egg whites with the vinegar and vanilla. Beat, continually adding sugar, until the mixture is stiff enough to stand up in peaks.
2. Shape the stiff mixture into small shells on cookie sheets. Bake in a 250 F oven for 50 minutes, or until light brown and firm.
3. Let cool in the oven. When cool, refrigerate for about 2 hours.
4. Put the raspberries in a bowl and add the kirschwasser. Chill this mixture thoroughly.
5. To serve, spoon chilled raspberries in the cold meringue shells.

Plum Pudding

Makes 2 puddings
Total time: 5 hours for preparation

Janet

We always have this plum pudding at Christmas. It's one of broadcaster Helen Gougeon's, and simpler than most.

6 eggs
2 cups milk
4 cups all-purpose flour
½ cup rum
1 cup seedless raisins
1 cup currants
1 cup finely chopped walnuts
1 cup dates, chopped
½ cup mixed peel
½ cup butter
½ cup suet, chopped finely
½ tsp. nutmeg
½ tsp. cinnamon
½ tsp. salt
2 cups breadcrumbs
Rum to flambé

1. In a large bowl, beat eggs. Pour in milk slowly, stirring all the time.
2. Stir in flour to make a smooth cream. Add rum.
3. Stir in raisins, currants, walnuts, dates, mixed peel, butter, suet, nutmeg, cinnamon, and salt. Mix thoroughly.
4. Knead in breadcrumbs. Add more breadcrumbs if the mixture is not solid enough to knead.
5. Place in two bowls. Put bowls on a rack in a kettle or steamer over 1 inch of boiling water and steam for 3 to 4 hours, replenishing water as necessary.
6. When cool, wrap and store in a cool dry place for several weeks.
7. To serve, steam again. Heat some rum in a warm spoon and pour over pudding. Flame.

Note: More rum may be added to the pudding while it is being stored. Also add rum when the pudding is steamed for the second time. If you can find 151-proof rum (sold in the Yukon, for example), it makes a larger flame. (Pierre nearly set fire to the whole place one year because he forgot I had handed him the 151-proof. Be warned.)

Maple Mousse

Serves 4
Total time: 1 hour   **Janet**

Maple mousse is frequently served to visiting foreign dignitaries along with fiddleheads, buffalo roasts, and Arctic char. This particular recipe comes from the *Royal Victoria Cook Book*, published in 1900.

1 cup maple syrup
4 egg yolks, well beaten
2 cups whipping cream

1. In a saucepan, pour maple syrup.
2. Stir in egg yolks. Heat until thick, being careful not to burn.
3. Remove from heat and chill.
4. Whip cream until stiff. Fold into chilled mixture. Refrigerate. Serve cold.

Raspberry-Banana Fluff ✗

Serves 6
Total time: 1 hour

Penny

This is the easiest and most nutritious dessert I know of – and yet it's so delicious that few can guess that the main ingredient is low-cal tofu.

2 cakes tofu
2 bananas
1½ cups raspberries
1 tbsp. honey
¼ cup Grand Marnier
Ice cubes
Toasted, grated coconut for garnish

1. In a blender, place tofu, bananas, 1 cup of the raspberries, honey, Grand Marnier, and ice cubes. Blend at low speed until smooth.
2. Pour into chilled dessert glasses. Top with remaining raspberries and toasted coconut. Chill and serve.

Blackberry Pie

Makes 1 pie
Total time: 1 hour **Penny**

One summer several years ago, our family rented three cottages on Galiano Island, off the coast of British Columbia. We spent much of our time picking and eating the fat, juicy blackberries that grew thickly along the roadsides. I remember one day when I made at least six blackberry pies. We prefer them juicy and messy, rather than the regular gluey cornstarch texture.

½ cup sugar
1½ tbsp. lemon juice
Dash cinnamon
¼ cup all-purpose flour
4 cups fresh blackberries
Pastry for 9-inch pie (see p. 186)
2 tbsp. butter

1. Combine sugar, lemon juice, cinnamon, and flour.
2. Sprinkle this mixture over berries and stir gently until blended.
3. Line a 9-inch pie pan with pastry.
4. Spoon fruit mixture into pie shell. Dot with butter.
5. Cover pie with a well-pricked pie shell or with a lattice.
6. Bake in a 450 F oven for 10 minutes to brown. Then reduce heat to 350 F and continue to bake for 35 to 40 minutes more, or until crust is golden brown.

No-Tears Pastry

Makes 4 large pie shells
Total time: 2 hours

Pamela

Mom and I used to leave the pastry to Penny, since ours always crumbled and we ended up in tears. We haven't sobbed so much since we've been using this recipe.

> **5½ cups all-purpose flour**
> **1 tsp. salt**
> **2 cups shortening**
> **1 egg**
> **1 tbsp. vinegar**
> **Ice water**

1. In a large bowl, mix flour and salt.
2. Cut in shortening with a pastry blender.
3. In a measuring cup, mix egg and vinegar. Fill with ice water to make 1 cup of liquid.
4. Tossing dry mixture lightly, add the egg mixture slowly until pastry comes together in a ball. (You may not need all the liquid.)
5. Cut the ball into quarters. Wrap each in waxed paper or plastic wrap and refrigerate for an hour.
6. When you are ready to use, bring dough back to room temperature before rolling.

Note: This recipe can be made in a food processor.

SNACKS

Cheese and Apple Melt

Serves any number
Total time: 10 minutes   **Penny**

Try these open-faced sandwiches for breakfast, for lunch with Curried Squash/Pumpkin Soup (see page 36), or any time as a tasty snack.

> **Sliced whole-wheat bread**
> **Unsalted butter**
> **Grated Swiss or Cheddar cheese**
> **Thinly sliced apple**
> **Cinnamon**
> **Raisins**
> **Sunflower seeds**
> **Salt**

1. Lightly toast bread; butter the toast.
2. Sprinkle a thin layer of cheese on the toast; add a layer of sliced apple and sprinkle with cinnamon. Add a second layer of cheese; top with raisins, sunflower seeds, and a sprinkle of salt.
3. Place on a cookie sheet. Put under the broiler until cheese melts and begins to brown.

Garlic Cheese Toast

Serves 1
Total time: 5 minutes   **Rico**

A great snack.

> **2 slices bread**
> **2 cloves garlic, thinly sliced**
> **2 slices sharp Cheddar cheese**

1. Lightly toast bread.
2. Place garlic on toast. Space evenly to ensure that no single mouthful will have too much – or, more importantly, too little – garlic.
3. Cover with cheese and place in a toaster oven or under the broiler until the cheese starts to bubble.

Cheese Dreams

Serves 1
Total time: 20 minutes   **Eric**

A taste sensation that requires a minimum level of consciousness to prepare.

> **2 slices bread**
> **½ cup grated Cheddar cheese**
> **1 tomato, finely chopped**
> **½ green pepper, finely chopped**
> **2 green onions, or 1 medium cooking onion, finely chopped**
> **Worcestershire sauce for garnish**

1. Lightly toast bread.
2. Cover each slice with a layer of grated cheese.
3. Spread with tomato, green pepper, and onion.
4. Place on a cookie sheet and put in the oven. Broil for about 5 minutes or until cheese bubbles.
5. Garnish with Worcestershire sauce to taste.

Salted Almonds

Serves 8
Total time: 45 minutes   **Pierre**

It's a tradition in the family to have these in unnumbered quantities during the Christmas season. My mother made them for me at Christmas and I've continued the tradition. This is the minimum number; it will last perhaps five minutes. You can never make too many salted almonds – there are never any leftovers.

1 cup shelled almonds
¼ cup olive oil
1 tsp. cayenne pepper
Salt

1. Place the almonds in a saucepan of scalding water. Leave for 10 minutes. Pour off the water and replace with cold water. Peel the almonds.
2. Put peeled almonds in a bowl. Add the oil and cayenne. Shake. Add salt to taste and shake again.
3. Lay the almonds on a flat pan and place under the broiler. When golden brown, remove from oven and let cool. Turn each almond. Broil the other side. Place in a jar, add more salt, shake, chill, and serve.

Note: Watch the broiler: the almonds burn easily. And chill them until they are crisp before serving.

Orange-Peel Candy

✖

Serves any number
Total time: 1 hour and 30 minutes   **Pierre**

This was a tradition, like salted almonds, in my mother's Christmas kitchen. Now it's a tradition in ours. Part of the fun on Christmas Eve is making things like salted almonds and candied orange peel – and eating them all up.

Peel from 4 to 6 oranges
2 cups sugar
½ cup water
Granulated sugar for rolling

1. Cut the peel into strips.
2. Soak strips in cold water for 30 minutes.
3. In a saucepan, bring sugar and water to a boil.
4. Add the peel and cook slowly for half an hour.
5. Remove peel from pan and spread on a flat surface. Roll each peel in granulated sugar.
6. Spread peels on waxed paper until cool and dry.
7. Eat it at once, or store in a glass jar.

Note: Some people remove the white stuff from the peel, but I've never found that necessary. The cooking time is arbitrary. The longer you cook it, the chewier the peel will be. Try not to eat it until it's cool and crunchy.

Strawberry Dip

Makes 2 cups
Total time: 10 minutes **Pamela**

Serve this at June garden parties, as a "stand-up" alternative to celery and carrots. Don't hull the strawberries; the ends are handles for dipping the berries into the sauce.

1 cup cream cheese
½ cup sour cream
½ cup cottage cheese
2 tbsp. frozen concentrated orange juice
½ cup fruit sugar
1 tbsp. orange liqueur (Triple Sec, Cointreau, or Grand Marnier)
Strawberries, not hulled

1. In a blender, food processor, or mixer, combine cream cheese, sour cream, cottage cheese, orange juice, sugar, and liqueur. Blend all ingredients until smooth.
2. Place dip in a fancy glass bowl. Serve with a bowl of strawberries to be dipped individually into the sauce.

Fried-Potato Sandwich

Serves 1
Total time: 20 minutes   **Eric**

Another taste sensation that requires no consciousness at all to prepare and even less to eat. If you are a person who enjoys weight-watching, you'll have plenty of it to watch if you eat this little snack regularly.

> **2 slices bread**
> **1 potato**
> **½ cup butter**
> **½ cup ketchup or steak sauce**

1. Toast bread.
2. Cut potato into thin pieces and sauté in the butter until soft.
3. I often relieve my boredom with this little dish by adding one or more mystery spices, which I do by closing my eyes and going to the spice rack.
4. When you feel you're satisfied with your spicing, place the potato between the slices of bread with ketchup or whatever.

Popcorn Snacks

Serves any number
Total time: 7 minutes　　　　　　　　　　**Peggy Anne**

Popcorn is the best food for one.
It's healthly and provides fun.

No Frills Popcorn:
　　Popping corn
　　Sunflower oil
　　Salt

1. In a small, heavy pot, pour enough oil to cover the bottom.
   Turn heat to high.
2. When oil starts to smoke, add popping corn just to cover
   the bottom of the pot. Lower heat to medium. Cover.
3. Periodically, shake the pot, up and down, back and forth.
4. When the popping stops, remove from heat. Put popcorn in
   a bowl and add salt.

Tamari Popcorn:
　　Make popcorn as above, omitting salt. Fill a spray bottle
　　　　with Tamari soy sauce. Spray on popcorn, stirring
　　　　with your hand. Be careful not to soak the popcorn;
　　　　just sprinkle on enough to give a little taste.

Honey Popcorn:
　　Make popcorn as above, omitting salt. Put 2 tbsp. butter in
　　　　small saucepan and melt over low heat. Add 1 tbsp.
　　　　honey and stir until both are liquified. Pour over
　　　　popcorn, stirring with a wooden spoon, until popcorn
　　　　is well coated.

Lemon Butter:
　　Make popcorn as above. Melt 1 tbsp. butter. Add the juice
　　　　of half a lemon. Put in spray bottle and sprinkle on
　　　　popcorn.

Note: I keep my popcorn in a sealed container in the fridge so
　　it won't get stale and lose its pop.

194

Microwave Surprise

Serves 1
Total time: 3 to 5 minutes   **Eric**

Being a nighthawk, I often eat meals after midnight. However, since I don't live alone, I must prepare my meals in total silence and often by flashlight, so as not to wake up slumbering loved ones. Under these constraints, meals must be prepared quickly and simply. By far the easiest meals for me to prepare are those that I find in unmarked plastic containers in the refrigerator.

1 container of leftovers (shake the container to make sure it isn't full of popcorn kernels or chocolate chips or something like that)

1. If you are fortunate enough to have one of those microwave ovens with the built-in brains, your troubles are over. Simply put the container in the oven, close the door, and press "genius"; it will know what is in the container and time itself. For the less fortunate, the time-honoured method of cooking the container until the lid blows off has always worked for me.
2. Once this is accomplished, simply get a fork and start eating a meal that could be anything, and just as delightful, too!

Peanut-Banana Crunch

Makes 2 open-faced sandwiches
Total time: 3 minutes

Elora

When Elora has a sudden attack of the mid-day munchies, this is what we make; it's quick, nutritious, and she can make it herself. It's good for the midnight munchies for grown-ups, too. Here's the recipe in Elora's own words.

Peanut butter
Half a banana
Sunflower seeds
Crunchy granola
2 slices bread

1. Get a bowl. Put in a bunch of peanut butter. Put in sunflower seeds and granola. Squish it all together with a fork.
2. Put it on bread with a knife. Cut it into little triangles. Now eat it all up!

Metric Conversions

In cooking, it is not possible to convert directly from one set of utensils to another, since the numbers do not work out to even measures in most cases. However, here are some approximate equivalents to apply when using metric utensils.

1 tsp.   = approximately 5 mL
1 tbsp.   = approximately 15 mL
¼ cup   = approximately 60 mL
⅓ cup   = approximately 80 mL
½ cup   = approximately 115 mL
1 cup   = approximately 225 mL

8-inch square pan × 2 inches deep = 20 × 5 cm
9-inch square pan × 2 inches deep = 22 × 5 cm
8-inch × 4-inch × 3-inch loaf pan = 20 × 10 × 7 cm
9-inch × 5-inch × 3-inch loaf pan = 22 × 12 × 7 cm
9-inch pie plate   = 22 × 4 cm

200° F. = 100°C
250° F. = 120°C
300° F. = 150°C
350° F. = 180°C
400° F. = 200°C
450° F. = 230°C

INDEX